WALKIN' THE MAT

PAST IMPRESSIONS OF ABERDEEN

Compiled by Andrew Cluer

Lantern Books

Registration 59368. Company Secretary Melville Watson, Esq., MA, LL.B. Storie Cruden & Simpson Advocates, 2 Bon Accord Crescent, Aberdeen AB1 2DH.

Other titles by the author:
"Former Norwich", Archive 1972.
"Plymouth & Plymothians", Vol 1 & 2.
Lantern Books 1974, 1975.

Author's Note:

These are some past impressions of everyday life not found in many books on Aberdeen.

The Aberdonians admire the city silently — seeing all and saying nothing. Like the glossy leopards sitting majestically unnoticed upon Union Bridge, they will remain as unknown quantities.

Overleaf.

"I have seen
the sunlight
and the moonlight
shine on the white
streets of Aberdeen."

"The Lollipop Lights of Union Street".
(Verse by Ronald Campbell MacFie.)

ISBN 0 9502853 4X.

£5.50 Net U.K. only.

Lithographed by Wright Printers, Dundee.

Dedicated to my wife Brenda.

A few words from David Duncan, an Aberdonian who contributed this poem as a frontispiece.

"ABERDEEN MY CITY"

Aberdeen, clean, grey granite bastion
Looking out towards the green turbulent
    waters
That wash-drench the rocky monuments
Off the bleak beautiful scene of the North
    East
This historic abode of countless generations,
People inured to privation — the storms
    blast
This community challenging the might of the
    deepwaters,
Garn bring the bountiful harvest with
    incessant toil.
This rich, enobled seat of learning;
Nurtured from reason —
The democratic Grecian art:
Fused by Roman principle and jurisprudence
(These) honed — matured — indigenous;
    culture . . .
The inborn talent — the lofty precept
The rugged, dour determination
That fashioned pioneers — Builders . . .
They gave God a lamp to cleave the dark
    powers
To its furthest perimeters.
This well beloved city honoured —
Made warm with pride —
Friendliness of a thousand generations
That gave it heart —
Enduring — Echoing its mother's love,
To call the exile on a foreign strand —
Enrapturing the mind with once homely
    joys —
Friendships welded in the salad years . . .
Aberdeen — Ancient City — renowned, now
    poised
For greater honour, greater ambition in
    modern times.

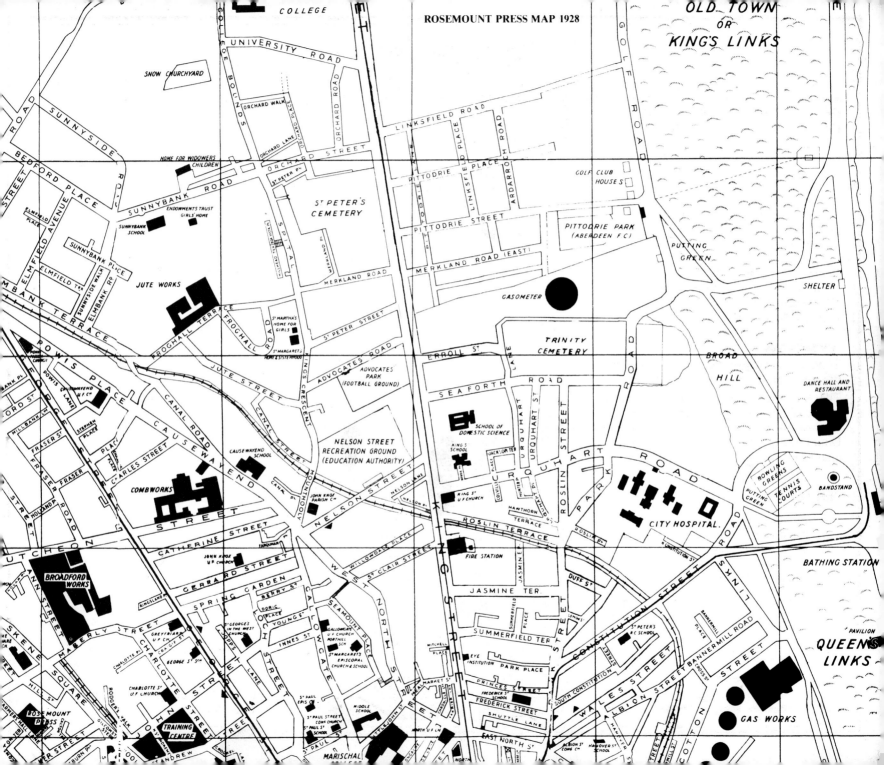

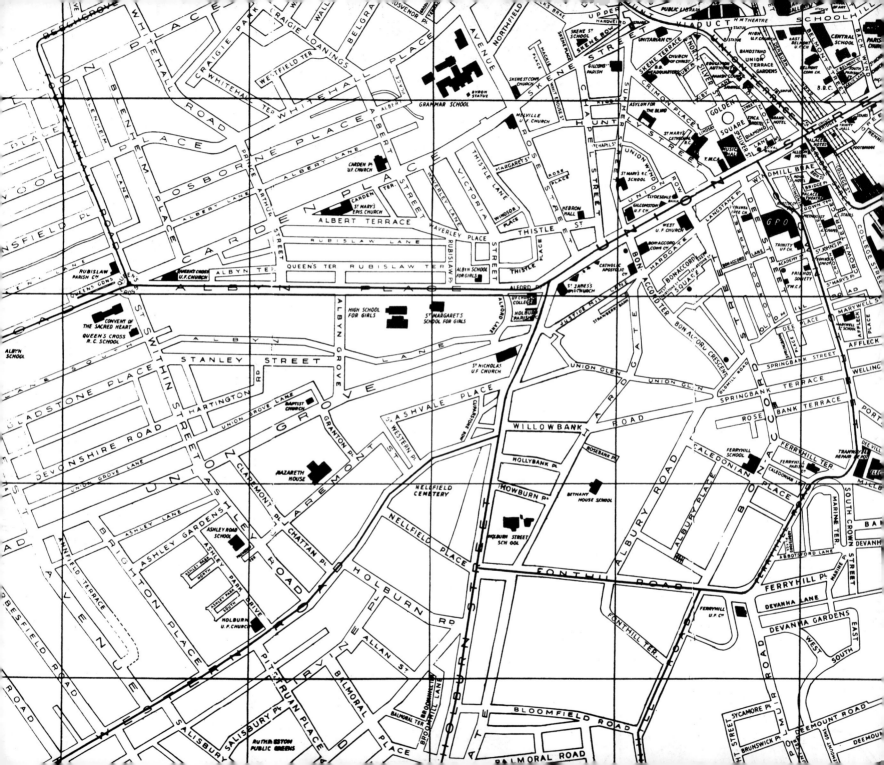

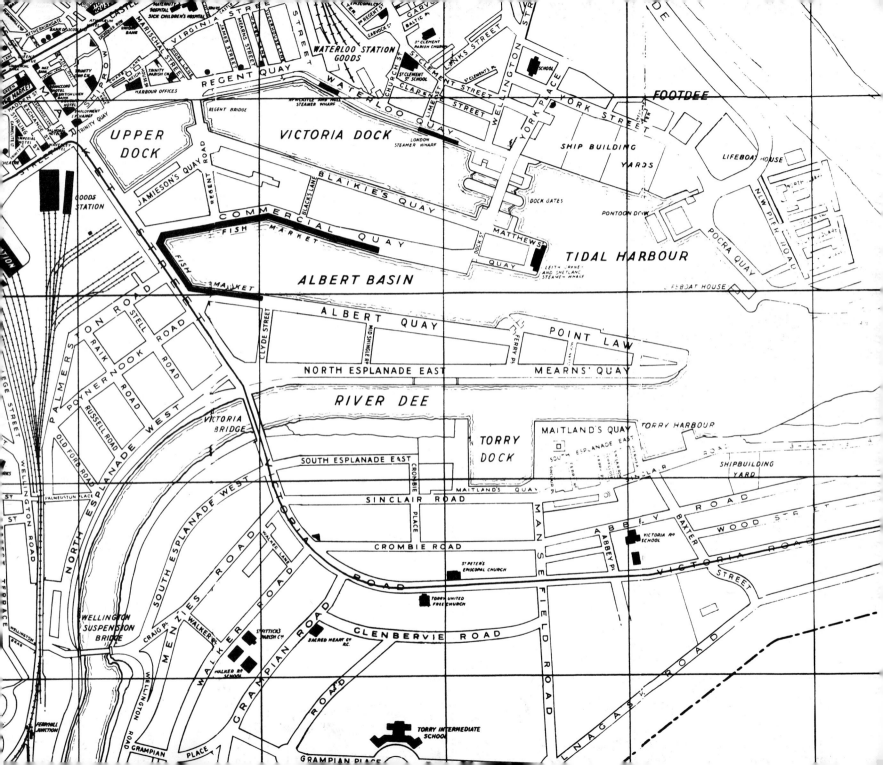

CONTENTS

Buddha collecting at Kittybrewster. Aberdonians have a high rating in the world as being unknown quantities.

ACKNOWLEDGEMENTS

"The Scaffies' Picnic", Bay of Nigg.

Especially to John Andrews of Kittybrewster, Aberdonian, *who provided some of the "stories that the professors didna' ken", and added a few that the cairters had forgotten. And to Jim Mackie who has contributed his version of walkin' around Aberdeen with a camera.*

With thanks for their kindness, patience and pictures: *Aberdeen Harbour Board (Mr Will), Aberdeen Journals, Aberdeen Northern Marts, Mr Bain, Bill Baxter, Mrs C. Birnie, Leo Blackhall, Sandy Booth, Bill Calder, John Bell Antiques, May Black, Misses Craig, Davie Duncan, Jack Esslemont, Finlay & Co., Alex and Daisy Gardiner, Hall Russell (Mr Tute), Mrs A. Hill, Richard Irvin & Sons, The Keith Family, J. Lees, John Leiper, J. H. Mackie photographer, Lewis L. Mackay, Roberta McCrorie, Norma and Bob McCrorie, Mr McLaren of John Fyfe, Gordon McGruer, Eleanore Middleton, Mrs Masson, Tom Moir, Northern Co-op (Mr Simpson), J. Ogilvie, John Reynolds, W. Ritchie, Mr Rust of Chas. MacDonald, Mr Shepherd (Davidson & Kay), Shore Porters Society (Mr Gordon), Robert Singer, Mr*

William Skene aged 96 (last saddler at the Brig O' Dee), Ada Smith (Harry Gordon's dresser), St. Margaret's Convent Spital, Jimmy Stevenson, David Stewart, Willie Stiven, Alan Stott photographer, Rodger Taylor photographer, Frank Thain, Trustees Aberdeen Masonic Temple, Ushers (Devanha Brewery Mr J. Hill & Mr Davidson), Georgina Wilson, Bill Wood & Staff, James Wright, Dinah Whyte, and to the many other people who have assisted me along the way. I apologise for omissions; however as Alexander Cruden mentioned in these pages, said of his "Concordance", "Poor sinful man can do nothing absolutely perfect and complete".

Gordon Calder, photographer and friend, worked on the book for two years.

Also assistance from the Librarians of Aberdeen: *Peter Grant, Esq., ALA, City Librarian, S. R. Lathan, Esq., FLA, Principal Librarian, Robert Gordon's Institute of Technology, North East of Scotland Library Services, Marcus Milne, Esq., Jim Duncan, Esq., MA, ALA, Moira Wilkie, BA, FLA,*

Mary Williamson, MA, ALA, Elma Garden, MA, ALA, Catherine Taylor, MA, ALA, and May Thomson.

Also to the City and University of Aberdeen Archives, *Ian Mackenzie Smith, Esq., DA, ARSA, FRSA, FFA (Scot) Curator of Aberdeen Art Gallery and his staff, The Department of Conservation Aberdeen City District Council kindly loaned photographs and John Soutar, FSA (Scot) Senior Planning Assistant also put his personal collection at my disposal. Thanks also go to The Country Life Archive at the National Museum of Antiquities, Radio Times, Hulton Pictures Library, and the Royal Commission on the Ancient and Historical Monuments of Scotland (The National Monuments Record).*

Professionally, to Stanley Robertson, Balladeer and Folklorist, *who contributed many items from his repertoire.*

A copy of the book acknowledging the source of the plates has been deposited with Aberdeen City Library.

THE GATES OF ABERDEEN

The Hardgate and the Windmill Brae,
The Shiprow and the Green,
Were then the only thoroughfares
That led to Aberdeen.

William Anderson.

History is embedded in street names, and Aberdeen's own street lore is alive.

THE BOOLGATE

(Later known as Albion Street)

FROM JUSTICE PORT and Park Street to the Links over "The Little Tarry Briggie". So called, because it led to a bowling green, from which the perilous shoreline between Seaton and FootDee could be seen. This is the subject of "The Bannermill Lassies' Song" . . . "Fan I cam' by the Salmon Fishers', fan I cam' by the Roperie; there I saw my sailor laddie, sailing on the raging sea." This important fragment of "The Bogmill sang-aboot" has overtones of "Captain Pugwash" and cardboard cut-outs; and, in fact, the tumble-down theatre was a landmark at the top of The Boolgate. A tenement which divided Wales Street from Albion Street was the childhood home of Willie Robertson's family, from whose singing, so many of the Aberdeen faces and places come to mind . . . afresh.

The Corner of The Broadgate and Huxter Row.

College Gate. The Waterhouse and Byron's Lodging in the Broadgate. (Site of Marischal College facade.)

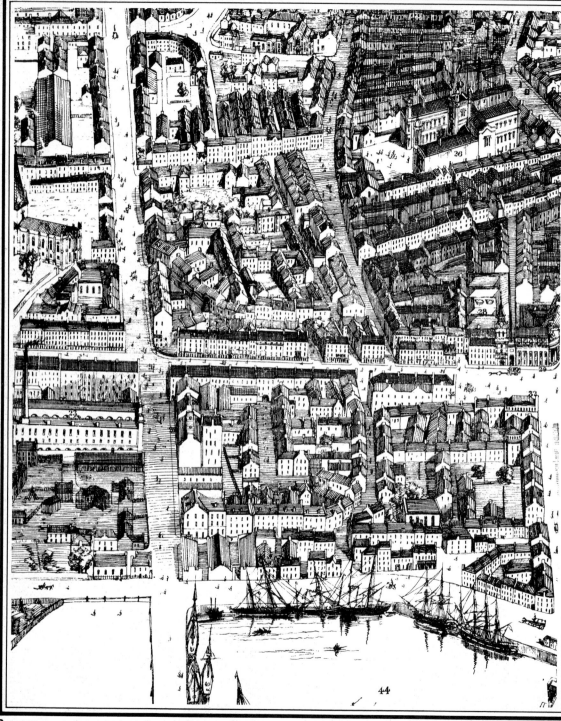

George Washington Wilson produced his first Bird's Eye View of Aberdeen from various towers and spires, a short time after the death in 1847 of the best remembered architect of "The Granite City", Archibald Simpson.

From the old tower of St. Nicholas Kirk, whilst periously close to the bell chamber, he sketched the huddled houses that contrasted with the new stone of the street improvements, which today have left the former "right little, tight little burgh" with only a few sandstone molars.

On the ancient roofs the slaters could be seen shivering with "hackit" fingers caused by the cold when they dropped a heavy iron ball and brush down the flues, sometimes at 5 a.m. so that a household might clear up before breakfast. Alec Booth, who with his sons were members of the fire brigade as a master sweep received sixpence per chimney and made his own brushes by dipping the bristles in hot tar.

 "Look at the fever-infested backies of West North Street."

The Mitchell Tower stands aloof above  the reeking lums of West North Street. Seamount Steps originally led to the windmill, and people passed the time of day admiring a sky shot with silver.

4

THE BROADGATE

From Union Street to Gallowgate

FORMERLY a shopping street that catered for the immediate needs of Marischal College.

Thirty shilling serge suits hung outside the outfitters at College Gate. In those days it wasn't the tailor's label that counted, but mottos were a sure sign of wisdom. Marischal College's motto still encourages intellectual good manners: "They have said; what say they? Let them say."

Students and professors crossed the quadrangle to the college gallery in the old Greyfriars Kirk. It was said of this arrangement: "Kirk and college keeping time, faith and learning chime for chime." The old building was hemmed in by houses fronting on to the Broadgate; hence the dark interior. Some folk were too feart to come here at night, because William Forsyth, a local journalist, had warned his readers about a gathering of ghosts in the Candlelit Kirk.

Muffled wheels no longer trundle over the wooden setts that oozed with tar collected by barefoot loons who played bools in the half light down "the street of a thousand smells".

The town's fire engines were originally kept at the Broadgate Waterhouse. This building had a clock by which "the young Highlander", Lord Byron (who lived next door but one at number 64), learnt to tell the time.

"As we were going through College,
all the boys were playing ba';
and there, I saw my ain true love,
the fairest of them a'—
and it's there I saw my ain true love,
the fairest of them a'—
He's my ain bonnie boy, dressed in blue."

(An excerpt from "The College Boy".)

Greyfriars Kirk.　　College Gate.

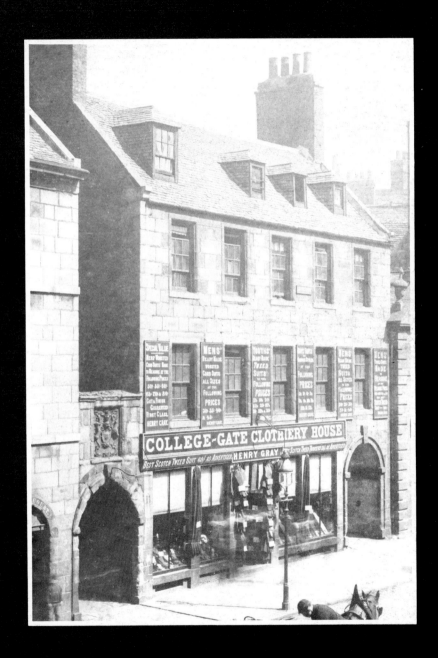

A Riddle

Come a riddle, come a riddle, come a rot-tot-tot;
A wee wee mannie in reid reid coat –
A stave in his han' an' a stone in his throat;
Come a riddle, come a riddle, come a rot-tot-tot.

(The Cherry)

IT COULD contain two regiments of foot soldiers drawn up in rank and file, and was just as crowded on Hogmanay night: "Get up auld wife an' shak yer feathers; dinnae ye think that we are beggars. We're only bairnies come oot tae play, get up an' gie us oor Hogmanay". Children used to play on the raised steps known as "the Plainstanes". It was a good place to see all the "East Neuk worthies", because the old post office used to be housed inside the Mercat Cross. When the mail arrived, the mail coach post horn was sounded and letters were collected. A hundred years ago, David Bannerman, the town's drummer, dressed in a red coat, still announced "losts and founds".

On Saturday night, "country giordis" were given "a penny worth of torture" from the electric shock wheel. Another meeting place was the coffee stall, and it was the custom "to hae a dander tae the market, and hae a rake aroun'." "Old claes", hardware and cracked pictures were on sale still at dusk; and the flares above the booths made it an exciting place to hear ghost stories, or listen to the impromptu concerts. At ten o'clock, the Salvation Army commenced "beating the drum, and saving the souls".

Farm servants were warned about the enticements of market stance and dram shop at the half yearly feeing markets. An old ballad called "shoval's Caie" tells how elopements were planned: "For soon it will be Martinmas, an' I will get my fee; for it's at Martinmas that she'll run awa' wi' me".

Often plans didn't work out, and broken hearted halflins were spotted by recruiting sergeants who came specially to markets and fairs.

CASTLEGATE

From Union Street to Justice Street and Castle Terrace
(The Castle Road of 1272, explains the history books)

"Twa recruiting sergeants come frae the Black Watch — Markets an' fairs some recruits for tae catch, and aye that enlisted were forty an' twa; enlist bonnie laddie and gang awa'."

"Are ye feed yet min?" asked the navy suited farmers who sported a double watch chain and gold sovereign box. They hastily hired their farm servants on "Muckle Friday" in May and September before the "halflins" decided to "take the King's shilling" and see the world with the army instead.

The last timmer market was held here in the original stance in August 1934, when most of the wares on sale were still wooden. Children were promised maybe a small wheelbarrow or rocking horse. Housewives stocked up with items essential to the tradition kitchen, dairy, farmyard or bothy. Brose bowls, ("caps"), porridge stickes ("spurtles"), ladles, rolling pins, pans, buckets, tubs, washing dollies, ladders, creel wands for basket making, and wooden shoe cleaning boxes.

A choice of food was offered for sale. Bargain bags of cheese cuttings, ham cuttings or chippit fruit helped folk to feed large families.

"Brongo" the public dentist stood with his back to the citadel. He talked engagingly to the crowd, so that before a child had realised it, the tooth had been removed with forefinger and thumb by the ex-boxer, who promised comfort to the crowd, if they purchased a pot of his own corn cure at sixpence a time. To prove how harmless the mixture was, he even savoured it on his own tongue. Dante's "sarseperilla tonic", herbs, etc., cured most other complaints, although Indian

A Riddle

As I wis walkin' by my lane
I met a man I didna' ken –
I cut aff his heid an' drunk his bleed;
and woke up next mornin' nearly deid.

("The first tasting of the wine")

aphrodisiac perfume which was decanted into little bottles from a half gallon jar, conjured up images far from familiar surroundings. It was at the Mercat Cross that the Magistrates celebrated their loyalty to the new Sovereign, after the proclamation of accession had been read, by drinking wine and breaking the glasses. On one occasion, however, this was not considered a pleasant duty. "We refer to the proclamation of the pretender in 1745, when the rebels, having failed to induce the Provost to drink, poured the wine down his breast". Historians haven't overlooked that the Royal Salmon dinners deserve a place in gastronomic annals: In addition to the twenty dishes of salmon cutlets, there was vol-au-vent of sweetbread, ten roasts of beef, four saddles of mutton, two rumps of stewed beef, six turkeys, six beef steak pies, ten lobster salads and twenty dishes of game."

Before The Royal Athenaeum was associated with feasting, it was a newsroom, where an old lady keeper tapped readers on the shoulder saying, "you've only put a bawbee in the box." (The extra halfpenny was received with a disdainful snuff.) The reading room didn't prosper, but when the place was taken over by Jimmy Hay it was transformed into a popular meeting place. "The restaurant", wrote Eric Linklater in 1929 was "black and gilded about the ceiling. The smoke of the richest, reddest steak in Scotland had darkened its mouldings, and ghostly vineyard perfumes haunted every corner."

Rolland's Lodging (number 38 Castlegate, on the south side) mystified antiquarians because the "harled hoosie" had "a sixteenth-century vaulted basement, open fireplaces, and aumbrys".

COWGATE

Justice Street to Park Street

ANCIENTLY, an old drove road to the harbour. It is last mentioned in the Directories for the year 1892, and there is no longer grazing ground at "Futty's Green Meadow".

"I come tae The Cross,
 an' I met a wee lass;
Says I, 'My wee lass are ye willing tae go —
Tae tak' share o' a gill?'
She said, 'Sir, I will —
for I'm the wee lassie wha nivver says no'."
> (An extract from the ballad,
> "The bonnie wee lassie wha nivver says no".)

A hundred years ago, David Bannerman, the Town's Drummer, dressed in a red coat, still announced "losts and founds", as well as public roups.

FITTIE GATE

A SMOOTH grassy stretch, by the shore-lands alongside Virginia Street, where the custom of "walkin' the carpet" (or "Mat") originated. Similar claims have been made for other places in the town where the grass seems greener to young Aberdonians.

The Market Cross and Record Office, Castlegate, whose contents are now housed in the gallery of the charter room in the Town House.

On the death of JAMES GRAY

Bon-Accord will mourn to-day
For her son that's passed away –
Passed away with armour bright
From the thickest of the fight!
He had points and he had parts,
That have gained the people's hearts:
He was champion of their cause,
Foe to all obnoxious laws;
Friend and foe had to admire
Bursts of wild volcanic fire;
Ever fearless, ever brave,
See the thousands round his grave;
Now that form they loved so well
Rests in peace in Allenvale.
But that form had a soul
Death itself could not control

Tell me Parson, if you can,
Where's the spirit of the man?
You have tried, but have not shown,
How to pierce the great unknown.

Market Cross by gaslight.

"As a shadow, so flits life."
Councillor James Gray at his daily
calling, passes the time of day reading
beneath the Tolbooth Sundial".

Timmer Market, Castlegate

This market-day we ill could spare,
  For though o' timmer unco bare,
There's routh o' smachrie, wealth o' toys,
  For merry-hearted girls an' boys.
An' here they come frae Brig o' Dee,
  An' Fittie Square doon by the sea,
Frae sleepy Aulton, brisk Woodside,
  An' Rubislaw, whaur the gentry bide,
Frae fair Rosemount an' Torry's braes,
  They come wi' hale an' clooted claes,
Frae Bawbie Law's an Split the Win',
  Wi' hurryin' feet an' deevin' din,
They rush in croods tae spend an' play,
  This joyous Timmer Market Day.
Time was, my friend, your heart and mine,
  Was blithe as theirs in Auld Lang Syne.

Cabbies counted their tips by the Market Cross. Young assistants were told that it could not be a half and half split, for, "The boss had the horsie to feed."

Market Cries of the Castlegate:
"Hard corns, soft corns, black corns, seedy corns, I cure them all".

"The morn's the Timmer Market, we'll a' be dressed in blue.
A reid ribbon in yer hair, an' a sweetie in yer mou'."

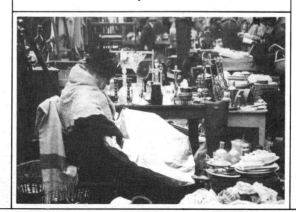

"Bananas all the way from the Canary Islands; bloody oranges from the Holy Land."

GALLOWGATE
From Broad Street to Causewayend

"YE MUST let folk ken that The Gallowgate wasn't a boring place at a'. I mind the clatter o' handcairts an' a babble o' tongues heard in the sidestreets hitting the Gallowgate – Ken Innes Street and Young Street. A' sorts o' interesting folk bade in Berry Street".

Screams of delighted children on "The Big Swings", known as "The waves of the Ocean"; and the distant hubub of the Guestrow carnivals was part of the lively spirit of the place.

The Old Market Stance, Castlegate.

Site of Mar's Castle, Gallowgate. The old Quaker chapel roof can be seen beyond the ruins.

Mar's Castle a sixteenth century lodging demolished in 1897. The Gallowgate Port itself stood nearby at the top of Young Street until 1769.

Gallowgate, looking from Mar's Castle towards the corner Co-op premises. Below this district ran extensive tunnels which were a source of mystery and terror to folk whose toilets were beside "the mouth of the catacombs".

"The Old Barracks" and Schools on the crest of Porthill. Now, even the famous hump at "The Top of the Gallowgate" has vanished.

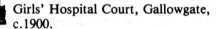 Girls' Hospital Court, Gallowgate, c.1900.

Gallowgate, looking towards  Mounthooly, c.1930.

The Gallowgate had everything going for East End folk; the Co-op Arcade, as well as a large variety of "sma' shoppies", open late on Saturday nights. Advertisements on the Corporation buses assured shoppers that, "all roads lead to Browns", (where penny packets of tea were sold to the needy). Nardie's fish shop and Bendelow's pies with their "fine het gravy" were local delicacies, whilst Greiggie's sweet shop was a "shoppie o' hert whaur sweet rations were issued lang afore their time." They sold "smush" from the boilers — the "chippit sweeties" left over after the home made "eens" had been put into the gleaming jars. Greiggie's cultivated a sweet tooth, because what they sold the loons and quines was "awfu' gweed". Customers were also sure to admire the collection of toby jugs that dated back to the time of "The Coughdrop Kings", sitting on the well stocked shelves.

"Pizzie" Grant.

There were plenty of broker's shops, where anything from a "demob suit" to tweed "plus fours" could be purchased.

Pawn shops were a sign of the more solemn side of life here, and an inscription under a clock of one emporium read "no tick here". "The Coopie divvie" was pawned for a half loaf, but somehow folk remained cheerful:

"Come and see my garret
come up and see it noo —
come up and see my garret
'cause it's a' mistrew.
A humpty backit dresser,'
a chair wi'oot a leg,
a three legged table and
and auld iron bed."

At the trial in 1876, of a man who stayed in Donald's Court, Gallowgate, it was revealed that his wife and six children were huddled into an attic nine feet by eleven feet. The contents of which were a straw mattress, a broken table and ricketty chair, chipped crockery; little else. Diseases like scarlet fever, and consumption flourished in such squalor.

My faither made a minister oot o' Tam,
and a teacher oot o' Jean,
but me he said, "A barber boy,
to use the Brilliantine".

Harry Gordon warned unsuspecting customers about a certain Gallowgate barber who "cut a bittie aff a mannie's nose," when he kept roaring for a hankie, he was told that "he had naething tae blaw". "Buckie Belle" would have provided consolation, for she sang, "my name is Buckie Belle, in the Gallowgate I dwell, I suppose you'll wonder fit I'm deeing noo; weel, I'm lookin' for a man be he aul' or be he young. Onything in breeks will dae me noo."

There was always a good film on at "The Globie" for them to see, and jam jars were accepted for the price of a ticket. Bags of mixed broken biscuits were available as cheap refreshment. Outside, the ragman shouted "tak' the stockings aff yer grannie's legs, the blankets aff yer mother's bed — toys for woollen rags".

Pizzie Grant was "a bonnie looking chiel" and has a special niche in North East folk-lore. As his portrait shows, he couldn't have been "the height of a bobbie's crossbar" — even so, he could carry weights of up to twenty stone. He was sadly missed by the "boorachies of loons" that went by names such as "The Causey End Rovers and the Gallowgate Rangers." He died on the roadside, walking back from Dundee.

The Porthill was the most northerly and highest of the three hills on which the "Braif toun" was built; and consequently the most exposed to the wind, which played freely round this echoing rookery.

Bairns would chant:

"Rainie rainie rattle steens,
dinnae rain on me.
Rain on Johnnie Groat's house,
far across the sea."

"The bottom of the Gallowgate", ☞
looking towards Littlejohn Street.

👉 Aberdeen has devoured the country between the Brig O' Dee and GarthDee Farm. Kaimhill children tended animals here as recently as 1980, and visitors danced under the stars to the loud music of the "Dogswallowers".

HARDGATE

From Bon-Accord Terrace to Willowbank Road, and from there to Riverside Terrace

SO CALLED, because it was passable, being the main road south and had a good surface.

Some of the houses at the Willowbank Road junction had the old forestairs, giving the place a village atmosphere. From the city stables, dung carts came over the pack horse bridge of 1654, which had no balustrades, so that large loads were not hindered.

Further on from the packhorse bridge, the river was forded, and the road followed the bank as far as Hildontree, then turning south through a peat moss.

The Brig O' Dee was begun in 1520. At the southern end where there was a chapel, and completed at the northern end, where there was a bothy used by the Hielan' fisher lads from Loch Maree.

🖐 Ruthrieston Pack Horse Bridge, Hardgate, near The Twa Mile Cross.

16

The Royalist defenders of Aberdeen (who numbered some 2,000 soldiers) lost the battle in the vicinity of this photograph. Lord Aboyne tried to outflank the Party of Covenanters, who appeared to be fording the Dee, at a higher point. "Bonnie John o' Pitmeddin" perished as the bridge was finally taken.

Some rode upon the black and grey,
some rode upon the broon;
but bonnie John o' Pitmeddin
lay gaspin' on the grun'.

Then up rode Craigievar—
says, "Wha's that lying there?
It seerly is the Lord Aboyne,
for Huntly wis'na here".

Then, oot did spak a false Forbes,
riding frae Druminer;
"This is the proudest Seton of a'—
the rest will ride the thinner".

"Spoil him", cried Craigievar,
"O, spoil him, presently;
but by my faith", cried Craigievar,
"He'd nae gweed will fir me".

They've ta'en the sheen frae aff his feet,
the garters frae aff his knee—
likewye, the gloves frae aff his han's—
they left him nae a flee.

Then they rode on and on,
and further on,
'til they came tae the Crabestane,
and wha' sae ready wis Craigievar tae burn a'
Aiberdeen.

Then up spak' the guid Montrose
(Grace be on his fair bodie!),
"We winna burn the bonnie burg,
we'll even lat it be".

"I see the women and children,
climbing the crags sae high—
we'll sleep this nicht in the bonnie burg,
and even lat it be."

The Ballad of the Battle at the Brig O' Dee, 1639.

Upon the eighteenth day o' June,
a drearie day tae see—
the Southern Lords did pitch their camp,
doon by the Brig O' Dee.

Bonnie John Seton o' Pitmeddin,
a bold baron wis he;
he made his will and testament,
a wiser man wis he.

He left his lands tae his young son,
his Lady her dowerie;
a thousand croons tae his dochter, Jean,
yet on the nourice knee.

Then oot cam' his Lady fair,
the tears did blin' her ee.
"Stay at hame, my ain dear Lord,
O, stay at hame, wi' me."

He turned himsel' richt roon' aboot,
an' a licht laugh gaed he—
"I wid'na for my lan's sae broad,
bide this nicht wi' Thee."

He's ta'en his sword, then by his side,
his buckler by his knee,
and he's lookin' o'er his left shooder,
crying "So'jers, follow me!"

He rode on, and further on,
unto the Twa Mile Cross;
and there, the Covenanters' shot,
it flung him frae his horse.

His name wis Major Middleton,
that manned the Brig O' Dee,
but it wis Colonel Henderson
that dung Pitmeddin in three.

17

"Trumpetty trumpetty trump,
the boys are on parade –
Trumpetty trumpetty trump,
the boys of the old brigade."

Castlehill, November 1934.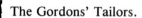

Fuentes-D-Onor.

Back Row Squad. Ptes.Lindsay, Wilson, Jamieson, Lorimer, 42 Grant, Matthews.
3rd Row. Ptes. Nish, McMillan, McKay, Lowe, Rennie, Dick, Wood.
2nd Row. Ptes. Kirkpatrick, 45 Grant, Gordon, Meddleton, Thomson, Smith, Skene, Dunward, Fraser, Winton.
Front Row. Ptes. Campbell, Johnston, Cpl. Perceval, Sgt. Aitken, L./Cpl. Milner, Ptes. Young, McCreery.

The Gordons' Tailors.

CASTLEHILL

CASTLEHILL WAS KNOWN and respected as being the home of the great fighting regiment, the Gordons. Quines who "wanted to be a Gordon's wife" peered through the railings to see the regimental tailors sitting crosslegged; at work making kilts, or sewing on ensignia.

During the winter, battalions training here were used to deep cuts in their knees, where the kilt swung, being kept open by the coarse material. On hearing of this discomfort, Queen Victoria directed that only pure wool be used by these regimental tailors.

"One day when I was walking in
bonnie Aberdeen, I saw the Gordons
marching in tartans gay and green;
beside me stood a lassie nae higher
than my knee, and as the lads ga'ed
swinging by, that lassie said tae me:
Here's to the Gordons, the lads who're
staunch and true! If I'd been a laddie,
I'd be a Gordon too, but seeing that
I'm a lassie, I must lead a lassie's life,
but one thing I'm determined on, is
being a Gordon's Wife".

THE JUSTICE GATE

From Castlegate, between the Heading Hill, and the Castlehill

THE PORT was built in 1440 at the east end of the Castlegate. Upon it were spiked the dismembered limbs of criminals. Nearby stood the Record Office, where the historic archives of the city were stored, until the new town house charter room was built. Picturesque houses with outside stairs led up to the Castlegate. These survived after the port was demolished in 1787, but later perished with the Victorian "improvements".

KING'S GATE

From Beechgrove Terrace via North Anderson Drive and "King's Cross", to Queen's Road

ALONG BRAE, where delivery boys back peddled their tradesmen's bikes. They spoke amongst themselves about the occasional introverted miser, here and there, that handed out a farthing as a Christmas box, only to have it promptly tossed back through the front room window. Neighbours' repartees were often the subject of merriment back at home after the rounds were completed: First wifie, "your front lawn grass needs cutting . . ." second wifie; "I have given my gardener a holiday." First wifie, "that will be in your garden shed at the back then."

NETHERKIRKGATE

From Broad Street to St. Nicholas Street

AN EARLY thirteenth century thoroughfare known then as "The Road of the Ashtree". Monks, and the retinue from Arbroath Abbey would be provided with "shelter, fire, candlelight, bed and clothing." Although the hospital of St. Thomas that received the poor and infirm was swept away with its gardens in 1770, you could ask for "onything ye wanted" at Raggie Morrison's bargain store, that rose from the site. At Aberdeen's own "Hudson Bay Trading Post," there were bundles of skins, frilly white nightgowns and enamel basins, bolts of material and carpets that were there on "the fleer", above which rose a spiral staircase in the middle of the shop; at the foot of which stood the haberdashery counter. Alert young ladies jumped to attention as customers approached, for they were paid on commission for every sale that they made

from threads, ribbons, tapes, elastic, buttons, and cushion covers to be embroidered. North East needlewomen still retain some of the supplies they invested in, even though "Raggie's is awa'."

QUEEN'S GATE

At the junction of Queen's Road with Forest Road and Forest Avenue

A TURNPIKE GATE, where heavy waggons taking Sunday School children up the Donside for a picnic treat, paused to pay their dues.

The toll keeper's cottage is still standing on the corner of Spademill Road.

Queen's Gate district is admired for its monkey puzzle trees and granite villadom, but a century ago it was open croftland as the name "Barefold" implies. The long low walls of that white-washed clachan stood on what are now the shaven lawns of Albyn school.

"Hirpletillim", a couthie name given to a group of pantiled cottages that only a century ago clustered around the spademill briggie, sounds as if it is a title of a Scott Skinner Fiddle composition.

UPPERKIRKGATE

From Broadstreet to St. Nicholas Street; but formerly extending to the foot of Back Wynd, (known then as Wester Kirkgate)

THE KIRKGATE PORT was pulled down in 1794, so there were no impressive engravings made of it with Marischal's minarets completing the scene. It was fashionable for merchants to live here at the "top of the Broadgait". This street had a number of narrow courts; and from the top of Ross's Court, the decrepit stair turret of Provost Robertson of Glasgoego's lodging

 Upperkirkgate, prior to the demolition of the south side. The Kirkgate port itself was pulled down in 1794.

(which had a concealed chamber in it), reminded readers of Robert Louis Stevenson's Ebeneezer Balfour and "The House of Shaws". Brown's Bookshop at the corner of Drum's Lane was more welcoming; it was always candlelit.

On a winter's night, songs, ballads and plays were displayed at John Hepburn's printing office in the section of the street now known as Schoolhill.

The mannie in The Wallace Tower niche "stood up to the queets in cement." This historic corner is now an impressive tower house at Tillydrone, and the couthie narrows of this arm of the Netherkirkgate are lost inside a department store. Carnegie's Brae, where the future Royal Academician served his apprenticeship to a house painter in the cellar shop under the Wallace Tower, still leads via "The Dark Briggie to the Green."

☞ Barefold Clachan, Queen's Road, 100 yards east from Forest Avenue and Queen's Gate.

A merchant's house, "Robertson's ☞ Lodging", Upperkirkgate.

WESTERKIRKGATE

(Later Back Wynd)
From Union Street to Schoolhill

THE MAGISTRATES laid out this street, which originally ran down to the Green, in 1594, on the west side of St. Nicholas Kirk – hence the name.

The magnificent Baroque monuments behind which stable hands watched these shadows being shuffled like playing cards by the sun, were regarded as one of the idle entertainments of this thoroughfare; another was "the town's music" being rehearsed at "the song school".

The gravedigger lived alongside his work in a little cottage sandwiched between houses that partially enclosed the graveyard. Inquisitive bairns who asked him about the

worthies in his care couldn't get the "Burking stories" or the ancient ballad rhymes out of their heads as they lay in bed at night thinking about their own funerals, and the grim looking white feathered hearses they had been promised, along with a driver with a white band on his hat":

> "Ding dong, . . . auld Lowrie's bell,
> Mary is my mither;
> carry me o'er tae the toun's Kirk yerd
> beside my elder brither.
> my coffin shall be black
> Six angels aroun' my back,
> two tae watch, an' two tae pray,
> an' two tae carry my soul away".

The Auld Lowrie bell was found in the charred ruins caused by the East Kirk fire in 1874, as well as a bible in which only one text remained legible: "Because ye have sinned against the Lord, nor walked in his Law, nor in his statutes, nor in his testimonies, therefore this evil has happened to you."

☞ George Jamesone's house, Schoolhill.

THE GREEN

**Anciently, from Windmill Brae to Putachieside and Fisher Row.
Now from East Green and Hadden Street to Denburn Road.**

"FRESH BUTTER, country cheese, eggs hot from the nest." Fruit-sellers at The Green sold giant cabbages grown on local allotments. Sir Walter Scott reminds us that the laird of Culrossie fought a duel for the honour of Aberdeen butter, and having thanked his adversary for his life added that "better butter than Aberdeen butter, ne'er gaed doon a southern thrapple."

The Cove fisherwomen at the top of the Green. On the left is Hadden's Mill.

Kirstie, Maggie and Kate, three Torry lassies.

Kirstie, Maggie and Kate, three Torry lassies started their day at 8 am, discussing new events and old times. Their "yella haddies and tasty kippers, tippence a pair, five fur fourpence" lay in baskets.

At the top of the Green, the Cove fishwives sold herrings from their creels. They were familiar figures seen round the streets in the evening with their black knitted shawls and murlins over their arms, selling any surplus fish before they returned home.

"Shoudie poudie,   "My Auntie Jean
pair o' new sheen,   she mak's ice cream
up the Gallowgate,   doon at The Green —
doon The Green."   My Auntie Jean."

The "Mannie in The Green".

Carrier "Parcel Sandy"
Between Aberdeen & Culter

DENBURN ROAD

From The Green to Woolmanhill

A FLEETING TRAIL of white granite dust was left by the heavy wheels of the horse lorries, that left worn furrows by the kerbside, as they braked sharply on the steep descent into a vibrating labyrinth.

The cassies were continually being worn down by cabs and two-wheeled milk carts, because the horses and carriers worked from four in the morning until seven at night.

"Parcel Sandy" who laboured for "Walker's Parcel Express" on the Peterculter run, fed and harnessed his own horses. Town horses slept in moss litter, and it was regular work to cog the horse shoes in the morning with strips of metal from syrup tins. He soon told the blacksmith, if he gave him cheek, that "yer cogholes are like yer mou'; too big, an' in the wrang place." Another repartee was, "chappie, the wheels may be roun' but the shafts are guy licht." Sandy worked late into his seventies, and never acquired a cart without bargaining for the rope to hold on the load. Leather-helmeted loons playing on the bucket swings in the Denburn Road Playground by "The Trainie Park", thought that he looked like a weatherbeaten old Red Indian. This was the carters route down to the station yard and Martin's Lane smiddy, so they hung on to the tailboard until a passerby yelled out "wheep ahin", and passengers were given a flick of the whip across the knuckles.

The Old Trades' Hall gateway, as rebuilt in Denburn Road. The inscription reads, "He that pitieth the poor, lendeth to The Lord, and that which he hath given will he repay".

"Parcel Sandy", the Culter Carrier, at the Denburn Road Depot, with a load of groceries and lengths of timber on board. His knuckles were red with hard work.

THE MUTTON BRAE

From Woolmanhill to Denburn

THERE are two explanations given as to why "The Brae" got its name. The first being that The Woolmarket was held nearby – the second being that this was the route by which the postillions took the carriages to call for the Belmont Street society women, who got themselves a reputation as being "mutton dressed up as lamb". Clachan folk encouraged their lassies to be humble and enjoy the simple things in life like "mony a

The full extent of Mutton Brae. The Triple Kirks as they were originally meant to be seen, above red pantiled roofs.

guid air" from the resident fiddler who would serenade them under "The Provost's Plane Tree" in "The Corbie Well Heugh."

DOOCOT BRAE

From the Denburn Bleach Green to "The Doocot"

THE NORTHERN ASSURANCE building occupies the site of the Doocot, but the present building is better known as "The Monkey House".

Corn grew in the fields where Aberdeen's New Town was built, and the pigeons filled their crops at the expense of tenant farmers only to replenish the larder of the Laird of

"Bonnet Laird".

Crimonmogate, when the *feu de joi* for the King's birthday was fired.

This vanished byeway gained noteriety as Sir John Cope's camping ground, but it was used by the Deeside and Donside Bonnet lairds whose shalts were tethered in the Denburn Wood known as "Corbie Haugh". Then, as now, the rooks are "nae bonnie singers", and the merchandise was swiftly removed to the Castlegate Market where they had a deal with the wrights and joiners for their planks and spars. They also had regular customers for their hazel wands that made creels, birchback for tanning nets, ladders, caups, ladles, spigots and faucets. Pine root firelighters known as "rosity reets" kept "mony a lum fanning".

Denburn Bleachgreen.

"YE BANKS AND BRAES" THE LOWER DENBURN

"IT'S NAE harangues we want, ye ken, nor literary scuffles, but lots o' sturdy willin' men supplied with picks and shovels".

Children once "made little pondies, and sailed little shippies "in the polluted waters of The Denburn, which flowed open through the centre of the city like a hardening artery, but it was the need for the Denburn Junction railway (1863-67) which prompted the above verse. Preservationists wanted an underground tunnel for the railway, because they liked the cascades and bridges that gave an impression, so they claimed, of a willow pattern landscape.

Archibald Simpson's Triple Kirks, (whose granite spire was clad in second hand bricks) cost the congregations of the Free East, South and High church, £5,000 in 1844. The architect overcame many difficulties with this commission, but it was his favourite work, and was introduced at his own request into James Giles's well known portrait.

When the railway was built over the course of the Denburn, a test to see if vibration would cause any danger to the Kirks' foundations necessitated tumblers of water to be placed in the doorways. "Whistling was not allowed as the train went into the tunnel" When the spire required inspection, James Wright, "the original steeplejack", who had scaled Britain's highest spire (that of Salisbury Cathedral) showed how swiftly he could proceed, once the two strings of his kite were on opposite sides of the Steeple, as he spliced on heavier lines to carry him upwards within the hour.

WINDMILL BRAE
From College Street to Crown Street

OFFICIAL RECEPTIONS and farewells to important visitors to the town from the south were made here, because then, Union Street and Holburn Street didn't exist, this thoroughfare which linked up with Hardgate, continued on over The Denburn, by way of the old Bow Brig, into The Green.

This route was truncated in 1850, for the Denburn Valley railway.

Nine years later the windmill was retired to "Drumgarth", a Deeside villa at Pitfodels, where "Johnny Cope's watchtower" of 1680 still stands sentinel, although the day when two thousand soldiers entered Aberdeen from the North in September 1748, has long been forgotten.

The city authorities never disposed of any moveable landmarks, and consequently, John Jeans' Bow Bridge of 1747 is preserved under the arches of Union Terrace Gardens, further up the Vale of the Denburn.

An ancient rhyme for a game called "beddies". The lassies and laddies faced each other:

> "There were three Dukes and a King of Spain,
> who came to court Mary Jane –
> but Mary Jane is far too young
> to marry a man of twenty one –
> she bows to the east,
> and bows to the west,
> bows to the one that she loves best;
> when she comes to the one that's true,
> she'll turn and say, dear, "I love you"
> But you're a' sae fat as barrels
> Sae upsy tupsy tee,
> o ye're a' sae fat as barrels
> Sae upsy tupsy tee –
> ye're a' sae thin as pokers
> Sae upsy tupsy tee.

"The Denburn Precipice", c.1850. ☞

THE AULD BOW BRIG

Each time that I pass by the bonnie Denburn,
When I look on its banks, it mak's me to mourn:
They hae biggit a hoose, wi' windows sae big,
But fit hae they dune wi' the auld Bow Brig?

There puir Mickey Gallacher, the sweep, di' appear,
And the loons on the brig seemed a' in a steer;
And black Alick Booth, wha danced mony jig
For the share o' a gill, on the auld Bow Brig.

There wis puir John Dickson, fan the brig he wid cross,
His stick graspit firm, and his head gaed a toss,
And the loons, ane an' a', frae the sma' tae the big,
Pulled his coat, crooned his hat, on the auld Bow Brig.

Puir black John Dickson told the head of police,
That for the loons on the brig he couldnae get peace;
Twa policemen were stationed, but they carednae a fig,
But teased him the mair on the auld Bow Brig.

There was puir bar'fit Jeams, wha the loons did torment,
Till ane aifter th' ither to the 'head place' he sent,
But each as they passed him they gave him a dig—
They were devilish loons on the auld Bow Brig.

When manhood approached them, they a' slipped awa—
Some gaed to the sea, some the plough for to ca';
Ithers went to Australia, their fortunes to dig,
And forsook a' their pranks at the auld Bow Brig.

The toon cooncillors came, when the loons were frae hame,
Tore doon the auld brig (oh! mair to their shame);
Had the loons been there, faith, "the man wi' the wig"
Durstnae touched but ae stane o' the auld Bow Brig.

But it's jist whit they dae wi' the puir workin' man—
Och, they tear him to pieces as soon as they can;
But stap them th'gither, wi' their bellies sae big,
They could raise nae sie biggin' as the auld Bow Brig.

The Bow Brig, which stood at "the fit o' the Windmill Brae", existed at the time this photograph was taken. Subsequently it was rebuilt as arches below Union Terrace, where old men hung up their rubber-tipped walking sticks on their favourite park bench, and fed the pigeons of "The Doocot Brae", who were accustomed to perching on "strang workin' han's".

Rosemount Viaduct, and the Denburn Road arch with Black's Buildings beyond, in 1886. Bridge builders carried milk cans with lids on, along with their ''piece'' to work.

Old Rosemount Viaduct.

Union Bridge from Union Terrace Gardens. The former Palace Hotel can be seen far right.

MACKIE PLACE
Off Skene Street

AT NUMBER SIX Mackie Place there was a haunted house known as "The Galleries". An intellectual group of people, who wrote poetry and journal articles, met there. They frequently got bored, so, dressed in white sheets, jumped out on passers by. Grotesque faces were carved out of turnips, the candles lit, and stuck in hedges around Cherryvale to frighten away inquisitive bairns. The town watchman didn't go further than the foot of Jack's Brae, so they weren't bothered. One of the carefree residents, Miss Forbes, wrote a few lines about the Denburn: "Beneath two giant willows that stand before our door, the Denburn runs so sweetly with its green and silvery shore.

But sometimes it is flooded and then the torrent's roar is like the sound near Buffaloe where hearing is no more; when down comes sticks and turnips, and tumbles down the wall.'

Oh! what a hurry scurry when you think the bridge will fall.''

SWINE'S CLOSE
From the foot of Jack's Brae to Skene Street

SOME UNOFFICIAL historians say that this short cut was named after the local piggeries. These were croftlands, and as the name of Hardweird implies, soil was unyielding, and consequently from ancient times pigs were kept in the district.

There can be no dispute now, because swine's close has been renamed Skene Lane. The Town's "ground officer visited a royalty stone here as he conducted officials around the inner city boundaries when they checked to see that none of the 'March Steens' had been moved.''

"YE BANKS AND BRAES" THE UPPER DENBURN

LEADSIDE ROAD

ON LEAVING the Dam of Gilcomston, the head of which was at Prince Arthur Street and Osborne Place, the Denburn split into two, and the old lade which gave its name to the locality ran along, quite open on the right hand side of what was a country road; with little bridges here and there giving right of way to those who had property on the south side. The road has been altered by the laying out of new streets, and the building of the Grammar School. The first bridge led over to the Model Gardens, a series of plotties, partially on the site of the playground. Immediately past this, another bridge led to Chadwick's woollen mill, the wheel of which was driven by water from the lade. The mill was burned down sometime in the 'fifties or 'sixties, and was not set working again. Close to the open lade near the foot of Short Loanings there were dwelling houses reached by a bridge from the north side. At the top of Jack's Brae the lade was covered, so that cart traffic could have access to the Northfield weaving sheds. Blair's Lane is the only survivor of the old courts of Leadside. The water of the lade drove the mill at the top of Jack's Brae, and again ran open, past what is now South Mount Street down to Gilcomston Brewery where it turned a large wheel and disappeared from view. Loons once searched for larks' nests in the fields where South Mount Street and Mount Street now run.

Honeybrae Farm, King's Gate. ☞

The "Fountain" in the old Fountainhall Road, now known as Desswood Place, was removed to Duthie Park in 1903. This one was originally one of six such structures, but in 1888 it stood alone.

STONYTON

THE SMIDDIE at "Stonytoun" clachan shoed the heavy horses that worked at Rubislaw. The trackway between the smiddie and the cottages led to the mansion houses of Fountainhall and Whitehall which a century ago stood in open country.

Stonyton clachan, on the north side of Carden Place between Blenheim Place and Prince Arthur Street, 1879.

"My mither mend't mi aul' breeks,
and woe bit they were duddy o';
she sent me tae get 'Mally' shod
at Robbie Thomson's smiddy o'.
The smiddy stands aside the burn
and wimples o'er the clachan o',
an' ilkie time I pass it by, I aye
fa' in a lachin' o.''

An excerpt from
"Robbie Thomson's smiddy"

HARDWEIRD

THE BURN ran open here, crossed by several bridges. Country women called to each other from opposite forestairs, as they gathered in their daily wash. Their men were often away with the Territorial Army; and the Stablers nearby hired out horses when the camp was at Montrose.

THE BAIRNS of the Upper Denburn played "leavio", "kick the cannie" and "hoist the flag". "Barley Door" was their favourite, and they all stood in a row – one would stand in the middle, and the object was to try and reach the opposite side without being touched by "the mannie in the middle". The last one to be touched was the winner.

THE LANG BRAE

From Skene Street, in line with Summer Street, to the Upper Denburn. Now an anonymous flight of stairs.

MISS CUSHNIE'S SCHOOL was at the foot of the Brae; when the burn was in spate, she was unable to receive her scholars. It is recorded that when "she bocht in grey peas and biled them" there were no absentees.

 Skene Street.   The Hardweird.

JACK'S BRAE

From Upper Denburn to Leadside Road

ECHOED WITH the clatter of looms; for weavers produced cottons, linens, haircloth and tapes in their sheds. This was a cottage industry.

"I wadna' marry a weaver ava, ava. It's pirns to fill at four o'clock in the morn . . ."

Weavers wore tall hats in which they could carry the pirns to the loom. On Friday they took "the wob" to the merchant.

STEPS OF GILCOMSTON

From Woolmanhill and Spa Street to Skene Square

APPRENTICE SHOEMAKERS who lived and worked in the tumbledown sheds known as "rotten holes" down by the steps, had to upturn their wooden brosebowls to prevent fouling overnight. Horn spoons were kept free of industrial and atmospheric grit. They slept on narrow bunks filled with straw, and laid down their weary heads on leather aprons that needed a sheen of hair oil to soften them.

 Looking up Jack's **Brae**.

Wordies' carters on their way to the  Woolmanhill horse trough.

Gilcomston steps and "the rotten holes". A tannery stood at the other side of the railway cutting.

"GILPIE" was known for its poets, penny shows and potted heid; but according to Dr William Barclay who wrote a very learned tract in 1615 on the curative powers of the Well of Spa Water (which was within earshot of Skene Square), that "barborous apothecaries, Highland leeches, mercurial mediciners and all those who could give no reason for their calling", gathered here.

TURNING OVER THE PAGES OF A GRANITE BOOK

M R GLADSTONE'S PLINTH was the pride of Wright's granite yard in John Street; for upon receiving the freedom of the city in 1871, he declared, "not a drop of blood runs in my veins except Scotch blood. A large share of my heart has ever belonged to, and will belong to Scotland".

Spital Granite Works — "94 men and a dog".

"Deeside Grey", "Bon-Accord Black" and "Balmoral Red" were all imported for monumental work.

"The Pynours", a dignified funeral service provided by senior Shore Porters. A Burgh minute book going back to June 1498 records that the magistrates gave them the right to carry seabourne goods at rates fixed by the council.

Monumental work was done in the outdoor sheds, with open fires keeping the men warm, but even so their hands froze to the shafts of their hammers.

THOSE THAT turned to the granite in the 'eighties would go to America as masons during "the coldspell", and work there in closed up sheds where the poor quality of the water helped to break their health, but not their will, for even with an injured leg, the granite merchant John Fyfe travelled by slow train to Newcastle in order to ensure that his firm got the contract for the granite work of the railway bridge.

Some sayings in the Granite trade

"A hert o' granite, and heid o' melon".

A doctor, an undertaker and a granite mason standing in a bar: The doctor, "I bring them into the world". Undertaker, "I bury them". Mason, reflects . . . "I pit a steen on top o' them to hud them doon".

Stonemason to apprentice: "If I had a farthing for every ton of granite used for building Aberdeen, I could buy the other half of the world".

Manager to apprentice: "How are you managing?" "Fine, here's me laying into this lump o' granite, an' it hisnae deen me ony herm" . . . Apprentices took a pride in the individual designs of each monument; for it was customary to throw drapery over a broken win in the yard, so that this detail was executed differently every time.

Many veteran masons' whiskers were in danger of being singed by "the bubbly lamp". Before mechanisation, sand was used as the first abrasive in polishing, and masons wore moleskin trousers.

A large workforce could be heard at the different processes that involved use of the pick, puncheon, single axe and six-cut bush hammer. Emery brought out the rich natural colour of the stone to their satisfaction.

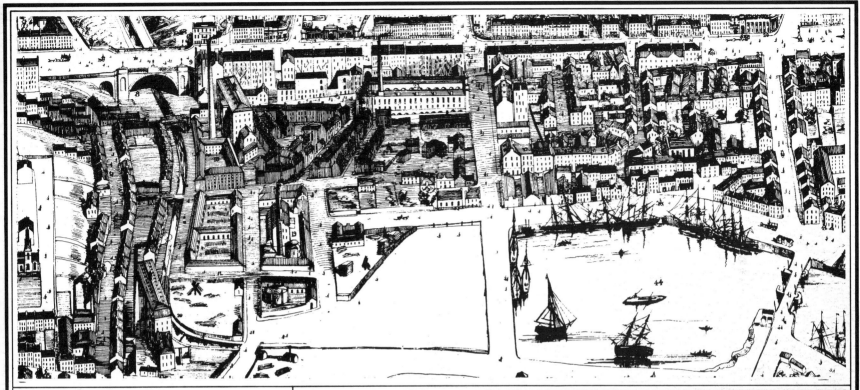

DAAVIT DRAIN O' HIRPLETILLIM
by "psalm-singin'" Willie Carnie

There's nae sic men a-makin' noo,
As ane I kent near Rubislaw Quarries,
His een are closed, cauld, cauld his broo,
He's deen wi' a' life's cares and sharries;
Daavit Drain o' Hirpletillim,
Drink never yet was brew'd wad fill him;
Stout an' swack, broad breist, straucht back
Gaed strength and swing to Hirpletillim.

C. McDonald's Jute Street Granite
Merchants, 1879.

Rubislaw Quarry was hollowed out of
a sixty foot hill. Half of Aberdeen had
come out of it in two hundred years
for it was 465 feet deep, 900 feet long
and 750 feet wide.

THE MERCHANT'S SON

A merchant's son, he lived in wrong,
And tae the beggin' he has gone,
He's mounted on his milk-white steed
An' awa' for pleasure he has gaed.

Chorus: *Rife fal laddie . . . aye,*
Rife fal laddie . . . ah.

A beggar wench he chanced tae meet,
A beggar wench of low degree;
An' he's taen pity on her distress,
Saying, "Aye, my lass, for ye've a bonnie
face".

They baith inclined tae tak' a drink.
Intae a public hoose they went;
They drank strong ale, and whisky too,
'Til the baith o' them got roaring' fu'.

They baith inclined tae gang tae bed,
And under covers they soon were laid;
The whisky gaed straight tae their heid,
An' the baith o' them lay like they were
deid.

Noo, in the mornin', this maid arose,
An' she's pit on the merchant's clothes;
Wi' his hat sae high, an' his sword sae dear,
For she's awa' wi' the merchant's gear.

Early the morn' the merchant rose,
An' lookit roon' for tae find his clothes;
There wis naethin' left intae the room,
But a ragged petticoat, an' a wincie goon.

Him bein' a stranger intae the toun,
it's he's pit on the wincie goon;
An' doon the street he strode and swore
that he wid never lie wi' a beggar no more.

The Tolbooth in the Narrow Wynd
was once known as "The Mids o'
Mar". The entrance to Lodge Walk
itself was on the King Street side of the
inn that the masons had built.

THE WYNDS

AEDIE'S WYND

THE WESTERN SIDE of St. Katherine's Hill. This "ski-slope" ran down from Back Wynd into the Green.

BACK WYND STAIRS
From The Green to Union Street

TAKE AWAY Back Wynd Stairs, and some folk would emigrate. This happened a long time ago to young loons who were supplied to American plantations as slaves. The last of The Green's medieval houses, known as Andrew Aedie's lodging, was known until its demolition in 1914 as "The Kidnappers House". Drummers and pipers were hired to muffle protestations from the barn nearby.

Is it possible that the art of Colonial epitaph writing has been influenced by Aberdeen's Own?

> "Sticks and steens
> will brak' my beens,
> but names winna harm me;
> but fan I'm deid
> an' in my grave
> ye'll mind fit ye caed me."

> Puir Gracie is deid,
> An' she lies in her grave . . .
> Lies in her grave . . .

> They planted an aipple tree
> Ower her heid . . .
> Ower her heid . . .

When folk saw festoons of apple blossom hanging over the kirkyard walls in Back Wynd

Back Wynd Stairs.

and nearby Correction Wynd, they told a cautionary tale about a youth wrongly accused of stealing fruit from the Toun's Kirk. Upon being interred in "The Pity Vault", rats gnawed him to death.

The funeral of Lady Anderson on 17th December, 1886 at the St. Nicholas Kirk seemed to signify the end of an age, when Sir Alexander, aged eighty-five, in feeble health, followed his wife's coffin to the graveside in a sedan chair, carried by two shore porters. A well-wisher asked the old Advocate if he was feeling better and was told: "I'll be no better laddie till I get to the Kingdom of Heaven", and turned away. He got there on 11th April, 1887.

CORRECTION WYND

From St. Nicholas Street to The Green

THIS IS THE only street now in use, that cut into The Green on the northern side, prior to the formation of Union Street.

Dr. Ferguson, the druggist, who had a number of creatures suspended in glass jars that could be seen through the window of his shop at the head of the green, encouraged children to bring him their grubs, piebald snails and dragon flies.

This was "a weel kent street", with a public soup kitchen at the Kirk. Coarse cloth was made by the inmates of the first House of Correction (1636). The Kirkyard wall cut out much of the daylight; advocates' offices in the garrets looked out over the tombs.

Correction Wynd, looking towards "the Beauvais apse" of the old East Kirk which was rebuilt in 1834, when much of interest perished, including "a large model of a fully rigged ship which hung in the sailor's loft, otherwise known as The Upper Gallery".

FUTTIE'S WYND

From Castle Terrace to Virginia Street

ONCE KNOWN AS Hangman's Brae. A convenient short cut "up the toon" for trachled fish wives. The story goes that whilst the Town Clerk was actively threatening redundancy to the hangman, the latter challenged him to a duel. Town Planning has belatedly responded, by cutting first, Castle Terrace, and later a ring road through the kailyards adjoining "the hangman's but-and-ben", thus executing Hangman's Brae. In the vicinity was Angel's Brae which ran from Castle Terrace to Commerce Street. There were no angels.

GARVOCK WYND

From Garvock Street to The Links

FORMERLY an ancient drove road that led from St. Fotin's Chapel to a watering place at the back of The Links. Now it is Lawrence Garvoc', a Provost, who is commemorated, not St. Fotin.

Futtie's Myre Croft House became Aberdeen's first Masonic Lodge building, and its thackit roof was at the mercy of tempests besieging The Heading Hill. This didn't disturb the members however.

Futtie's Myre thackit croft hoose, alias The Masonic Lodge.

NARROW WYND

THIS WAS THE Southern approach to the Castlegate, and was finally cleared in 1867. It's name had been given to a friendly society founded in 1660. Those who met there included silk dyers, soap boilers, flax dressers, saddlers, skinners, coach makers, farmers and stay makers, who paid the annual subscription of two shillings, a crown upon their wedding, and a shilling for each child of their marriage.

RENNIE'S WYND

From The Green to Trinity Street

A MILL STREET out of a painting by L. S. Lowrie. This was the Denburn Carters' route to the station yard.

ST. KATHERINE'S WYND

From Union Street to Netherkirkgate

IT IS NAMED AFTER the hill, effectively reduced by Georgian navvies, who also cleared an island wedge of buildings known as "The Round Table" when Union Street was constructed.

WINDY WYND

From Gallowgate to Spring Garden

A TRACK THAT followed the Northern bank of the dwindling Loch of Aberdeen. This explains the presence of a "spring" at adjoining Spring Garden, which has neither any delightful family associations with the singer Mary Garden; nor is it verdant any more with its derelict and "dark satanic mills".

DUBBIE ROW

From Putachieside to St. Nicholas Kirk

DUBBIE ROW can be no longer found. It was a hazard for man and beast alike, as the waggons rambled down to the harbour. As recently as 1865, the loch stream provided power for a meal mill, but even it runs unseen now below ground to "The Dark Briggie". It seems appropriate that the first Victorian braille handbook "Light on dark paths" to be printed in the city was compiled in the locality of Old Dubbie Row.

EXCHEQUER ROW

From Castle Street to Shiprow

THE STREET of The Mint — a narrow thoroughfare into which the sun seldom penetrated. The houses towered above The Quays like the enormously high old "Lands" of Edinburgh, and when Robert Burnett's house was demolished in 1896, a carefully built vaulted passage to the shore was found. Burnett, a merchant, held high office, but obviously was prepared to encourage illicit bargaining with seamen who knew the ways and means of manipulating the coasting trade.

Guestrow looking towards Netherkirkgate.

"It's half twal'." The night patrol shouted out the quarter hours and a weather report.

"Big feet, bap feet —
hear the bairnies cry
every ilkie morning
when they're plodding by —
They're chappin' at yer windies,
and crying through yer lock,
are a' youse bairnies in bed
its past eight o'clock."

THE ROWS

FISHER ROW

From the Green to Shiprow

THIS WAS THE now vanished route to old Trinity Hall from the Green. A narrow thoroughfare which was a short cut from the main road south, to the Shiprow; skirting the old boatyards. Snacks were served by the kerbside here: "Caller delse tae cha', a penny a bowlie". This was tender long tungles of seaweed that hissed as it cooked in a blackened iron pan, as "wee beasties" were scorched with a hot poker and served with vinegar and chips.

GUESTROW

From Netherkirkgate to Upperkirkgate

THE GUESTROW was one of the earliest streets in Aberdeen (1439). Although it was a narrow thoroughfare, it was never part of a larger Broadgate, because a burn ran between them.

In academic circles, the street became a by-name for good printing. Students, who didn't study their set books, were found in the underground shooting Gallery, where they passed the time of day with hardened Carriers, who stopped by at Mother Robertson's New Inn for their two-penny nips of "Kill the Carter" raw whisky.

"Shooting for spoons" preceded the era of the Guestrow Carnivals. The decor of the gallery was painted wooden panels, like stage scenery. In October 1932, Mr Fraser, the City Librarian heard of its impending demolition, and interviewed "a pleasant faced person about thirty, wearing spectacles, who in answer to his questions, said, "It's been an old house since ever I remember, the shooting gallery wis afore my time". He wrote down the pleasantries in his notebook. How long had she lived there? "A' my days", she answered. "You were born here?" "Aye, wis I that", she replied.

Courtesy to strangers didn't pass with the going of the Provosts and Dukes. "The Gush", as it became known, never sent the needy away without meat: "We'll give ye a crust but nae saxpence", was their saying. The House of Refuge was opened at Cumberland House here, in Spring 1836 . It's objects were expressed by Mr Brown of St. Paul's church Gallowgate, who hoped that this would be "a temporary shelter for the destitute, when hopeless poverty unsupported by moral principle first begins to whisper the possibility of successful crime"; and to give them once more "an opportunity" with all the concomitants of affectionate persuasion, and all the inducements of a fostered self-respect, to choose between the present rewards of virtuous industry and the agonizing consequences of dissolute idleness . . ." Under the watchful eye of Elizabeth Pirie, inmates could cook their own food, be their own waiter, and afterwards their own host and guest in the kitchen. Upstairs the beds were lumpy, and do-gooders were oblivious to the dis-comforts. "It should have been the 'ghaists' of these 'puir' folk that the street was named after, not the toffs with headstones in yonder kirkyard of St. Nicholas."

Funerals in the Guestrow were an event which attracted a great amount of public notice in Aberdeen. When Duncan Campbell McKinlay better known as "Blin' Bob" died, March 8th, 1889, thousands of spectators turned out. Mr Max Gregor, Marischal Street, took a plaster cast of McKinlay's head which was found to be 23½" in circumference. Had he been possessed of eyesight and education there was no doubt that he would have been a man holding a good position.

On the site of St. Nicholas house was Robert Reid's tobacco factory, where "the twists were bound with rope, smeared with treacle and pressed".

"The Ironmonger's Mask" was a reminder of a quarrel between two rival tradesmen. Alexander Stephen is now firmly fixed to the tower of Provost Skene's house. The other Russett sculpture has vanished. The scavengers of Aberdeen could keep out the cold with "a bowlie of soup or a mask o' tea" thanks to Russett's munificence.

From The Guestrow, "twa weel kent lanes" connected with The Broadgate; namely "Ragg's" and "Blairton".

HUXTER ROW

From Broad Street to Castle Street

THE BOOTHS in which dealers used to display small articles for sale gave this historic street its name. Huxters were issued licenses at the Courtroom here to carry goods on their back. On 26th January 1867 eviction notices were served on the residents, and a lady appealed to the Lord Provost, magistrates and councillors to let her take away "the almost indispensible commode, my water closet, which would be of little value to the said Gentlemen and might be very useful to me."

The original Lemon Tree Hotel stood here, but with the labyrinth of courts it perished when the Town House was built (1867-1872). Aberdeen had a very active book-selling and publishing profession, and the suppers were held in homely surroundings at the Hotel, and disbanded when the night patrolman, who used as his base the old watch house nearby, shouted "its half twal", adding the quarter hours and a weather report for good measure, so that Highland sheep stealers at Lodge Walk gaol nearby didn't loose contact with the outside world.

ROTTEN ROW

From Union Street to Guestrow

MORE PROPERLY known as Union Lane. It was obsolete wooden ships that were moored mid-channel in the Harbour that were known unofficially as "Rotten Row".

SHIPROW

From Union Street to Trinity Corner

"**T**HE PROVOST stood at the door of his house, and he counted his ships on the tide". Shipmasters and shoreporters lived here in sight of ships, and from Provost Ross' house, a clear view of work on board can still be seen. John Ross, the provost after which the early seventeenth century house is named, actually took up residence in 1782. This was a sprightly street, and sea shanties were played here by "the blind fiddler who lived in a house with a shipsign." Children cooled themselves in spray, as the "water-cairts" hosed down greasy "cassies". It wasn't their squeals that were heard, but those of horses at the vetinary smiddy, where there was a set of stocks to dock the tails. At the same time teeth were filed and a twitch put through their noses. "Dead dogs in the iron box were removed by the scaffies". No history of Shiprow would be complete without mentioning "the forty pots", which was a public lavatory with every claim to be as famous as Ali Baba's cave. "Trinity Corner", at the foot of the Shiprow, was a famous landmark that was claimed for re-development. "Tarnty Ha'" the eerie-looking home of the Aberdeen Incorporated Trades was cleared away, but the historic gateway of 1633 was moved to be the Denburn Road entrance of the Gothic Hall they built in Union Street.

College Gate, Broad Street. 👉

Mary Brooksbank, who penned the Dundee Mill Songs, was born here mid-December, 1897, into a grim round of shared poverty, hunger and hardship. Her father, one of the founder members of the Aberdeen Dockers' Union, was himself a dock labourer; her mother worked as a domestic servant when she wasn't a fisher lassie.

In Mary's modest autobiography, she allows the soft light from a pair of cherished brass candlesticks that cast strange shadows on the roof and corners of that well-scrubbed tenement kitchen, to linger on for posterity: In her own mind's eye, she could still see that light "shining down on the faces of our beloved dead", laid out on "the big brass-knobbed bed" in which she had fought off her childhood ailments.

At the age of eight, her family left "The Shore" of her "Grey City", on the *Princess Maud*, which plied between Aberdeen, Leith and Dundee. Dundee also claimed another native of Aberdeen, the remarkable Mary Slessor from Mutton Brae, whose achievements as a missionary in West Africa have been the subject of several biographies.

A discarded heraldic panel from a lofty merchant's house in Exchequer Row, which was demolished in 1896.

"AT THE FIT O' THE PEACOCK CLOSE"

"THE TOON had then but ten short streets; to ilka hoose there wis a yaird. But these auld yairds grew sturdy reets, an' ilka gate had aye its gaird."

Some courts were sketched or photographed, because of their ancient looking tower houses – "cleanlie and beautiful, neat both within and without. Most of them were four storeys high (some of them higher), slated and built of stone", wrote Parson Gordon.

After 1745, the ancient back garden ground was built over, and congestion occurred in these "pends". The introduction of the Police Act in 1795 meant that there was systematic naming and numbering of streets and courts. Some of the closes bear the personal names of feuars or proprietors, and this is an aid for those tracing their family history.

Some of these "closies" have fearsome ghost stories associated with them: An Aberdeen psychic has seen the menacing figure of a lynx-eyed, young priest looking out of a window, high up in the adjacent Poors House by New St. Paul's Church, and has felt compelled to follow him down a stone spiral staircase inside the building, arriving somehow at the derelict, chimney-dominated back lane of the long-demolished Dingwall's Court, by the Lochside. Whether the body of an Irish travelling lassie, who the man secretly murdered (and knows that the psychic knows), will ever be unearthed, remains to be seen; but, is it just a coincidence that, prior to his death in 1758, Mr Bisset of St. Nicholas' Kirk charged the Jacobite congregation of Old St. Paul's as being of "The House of Satan"?

Chapel Court, Gallowgate. 👈

BROAD STREET COURTS

CONCERT COURT, BETWEEN 10 and 12 BROAD STREET

The eighteenth century Aberdeen Musical Society used to meet here. This is the last of the Broad Street Courts.

CRUDEN'S COURT, 22 BROAD STREET

Alexander Cruden, author of "The Biblical Concordance" stayed here.

HENDERSON'S COURT, 46 BROAD STREET

A tenement tower house, now destroyed.

CASTLEGATE COURTS

THE CASTLEGATE COURTS were as vital to the Castlegate as the warm tar between the cassies.

The Annands, who documented the city life of Glasgow, never turned their attention to Aberdeen, so ill-lit stable courts, pends, vennels and closes have slowly gone out of existence: Albion Court, Bursar's Court, Commercial Court, Daniel's Court, Duncan's Court, Lobban's Court, Matheson's Court, Milner's Court, National Bank Court, Pirie's Court, and Smith's Court are no longer household names.

Harry Gordon immortalised Peacock's Close, where the city's dancing master stayed. An old ballad refers to it also. (There are two versions: one for "The Overgate" in Dundee, and other for "The Peacock Close" in Aberdeen.)

"I asked her whit her name might be, she says Jemima Rose, and I bide in wi' Berry Lane, at the fit o' the Peacock Close."

THE ADELPHI

The Adam Brothers' name is synonymous with the elegance of their own Thameside development, The Adelphi Buildings. Stone was sent by them to London from Aberdeen as a ballast cargo, to construct a classical labyrinth, that was later surpassed by the scale of the elevated arches on which Union Street is built.

The Aberdeen Adelphi was laid out on the crest of St. Catherine's Hill, above Ship Row, but approached between 49 and 51 Union Street; it is a cul-de-sac, and with its cassies, there is yet the feeling that the visitor could be entering a roofed-in Victorian Folk Museum. Here George Leslie printed a braille musical alphabet, and James Matthews pored over working drawings of Victorian Renaissance granite buildings, wearing a large bow tie and gold rimmed spectacles that added a touch of professionalism.

Rolland's Lodging, "The hoose o' the Maisters o' the King's Mint", Castlegate.

Rolland's Lodging (viewed from back court), 38 Castlegate, on the south side, mystified antiquarians because the "harled hoosie" had a sixteenth-century vaulted basement, open fireplaces, and aumbrys.

EXCHEQUER ROW COURTS

BURNETT'S CLOSE, EXCHEQUER ROW

Named after a seventeenth century merchant from Elrick. Affleck's tavern with its vaulted cellar stood here, and it was described as "the most recherché eating room in the North East of Scotland." (Demolished 1896.)

STRONACH'S CLOSE, EXCHEQUER ROW

Robert Stronach, a wright, used to collect shells off the beach, and carry them home in the deep pockets of his blue great coat. He painted them various colours and decorated the walls of his tenement with grotesque patterns. Hence, the place was better kent as, "The Shally Close".

"Airing Day", Exchequer Row.

"We're a' Jock Thamson's Bairns": a Guestrow generation game.

GALLOWGATE COURTS

CHAPEL COURT, 61 GALLOWGATE

Archibald Jaffray of Kingswells designed the archway here, in 1720, which is made of Loanhead granite, along with Old St. Paul's Episcopal Chapel, by the Lochside. J. Russell Mackenzie was responsible for the equally austere New St. Pauls, in 1867.

FERGUSON'S COURT, 30 GALLOWGATE

The order of St. Margaret's sisterhood who tended to the poor in their own houses set up their office here in 1864.

Until 1905, when it was demolished, Orphans stayed in "The Girl's Hospital", an old mansion of 1787 originally designed by William Dauney (Uncle of Archibald Simpson) for Gilbert Gerrard advocate. Mary Robertson, mother of John Anderson "The Wizard of the North", was kindly to the lassies, as her tombstone tells: "Yes! She had friends when fortune smiled; it frowned — they knew her not! She died, the orphans wept . . ."

REID'S COURT, 34 GALLOWGATE
(Otherwise known as Mar's Castle, which was built in 1494)

"Two tenements of foreland, and tenement of inland, with the close garden summer-house and office houses". The boundary of the garden on the South was where the society of friends had their Meeting House and their burial yard.

"Cumberland House", alias the  "Victoria lodging house". It may have looked like a castle from the outside, but the inmates shivered in an upstairs room, and lay on uncomfortable beds, gazing up at the mouldering crucifix patterns on the ceiling.

GUESTROW COURTS

BARNETT'S CLOSE
(From Guestrow to Flourmill Brae)

Here was the Aberdeen Dispensary and Vaccine Institution, which was inaugurated in 1823 for the purpose of supplying advice and medicine to the sick poor.

This close, with the trees, looking towards St. Nicholas Kirk, had a lot of character.

Rubislaw House stood in Queens Road, and was also owned by the Skene family. It

"Pit yer feet roun' the Kypie".
Playing bools outside Provost Skene's House. There were different types of bools: "cannons" (double shots), "mexies", "changies", "wateries", "tattie mashers", "ironers" and "claysers".

was demolished in 1886, and their town residence only just survived the Guestrow clearances.

Two newly weds took a room in the Guestrow, and were concerned that when they put down new lino there appeared a red splash by the window. One night they heard a tap tap tap at the window and not a soul was to be seen. On enquiring further, they found that a woman had been murdered there.

> "It's twal' o'clock,
> the ghaist appears;
> we'll a' ging doon the stair —
> an' fan we see the bogie man
> we'll get an awfu' scare."

Agnes Divie's house, in Galen's Court, 18 Guestrow, dated back to 1673, and the gateway arch to it stood next to Tam Gibb's Bar.

> It's a life, it's a life;
> It's a weary, weary life.
> It's baitter tae be single
> than tae hae a married wife.

> One says, "Marmie,
> gie us a piece an' jam";
> The ither says, "Deddie,
> gie us a hurlie in a pram".

Skipping song:

> "My mither says I mun go
> wi' my faither's dinner o'.
> Chippit tatties, beef an' steak,
> twa reed herrin' and a bawbie cake".

"Maria Bannerman's Grave" — one of the folk-lore traditions of Guestrow was dispelled when this survival of the Quaker's Cemetery was found to be a trough.

Looking towards the gateway arch to the house of Andrew Thomson, advocate, and his wife, Agnes Divie, as it stood before the Guestrow clearances.

Child sweeps, who hardly ever saw the light of day, found it a "sair fecht" to clean the crooked lums of the houses, which backed on to nearby Broad Street, opposite the archway.

Children sat on the steps of this seventeenth century "tenement of inland" at Mitchell's Court, 41 Guestrow.

SHIPROW COURTS

OLD TARN'TY HA' COURT

Old Tarn'ty Ha' was where the Seven Incorporated Trades met, until 1857, when they moved to Union Street because their land was required for railway development. The kirkyard of Trinity Hall Chapel was made into a boatyard as early as 1609, the year they launched the *Bon-Accord*.

Mary Brooksbank lived in one of the candlelit tenements of Shiprow.

Old Trinity Hall, "at the fit o' The Shiprow".

Aberdeen's answer to "Cleopatra's Needle", seen here in its original position, adjacent to Old Greyfriars Kirk, Marischal College quadrangle.

"Professor Beattie's House". He kept a "Commonplace Book" between the years 1773-1798, noting down the cost of everyday living and his other comments are a vignette of Aberdeen (which have been published by the Spalding Club): His lectures on moral philosophy at Marischal College nearby, and his poetry, won him wide acclaim. He wrote "The Minstrel", for he was a gifted musician — "when the gentle-eyed scholar played Scotch airs on his cello, he drew tears from the actress Mrs Siddons."

UPPERKIRKGATE COURTS

CHARLES COURT, 44 UPPERKIRKGATE

On the north side of Upperkirkgate; was said to have been called after Charles II.

DRUM'S COURT

A name, along with Donald's Court which featured a colonnade and service loops was a solution offered by the George Street Traders Action Group (GAG) to the problems of Town planning.

"Queen Mary, Queen Mary
My age is sixteen,
My father's a farmer in younder green.
He's plenty o' money to dress me in silk,
Yet nae bonnie laddie will tak' me awa.
Tak me awa, tak me awa,
Yet nae bonnie laddie will tak' me awa".

LOCHLANDS BAIRNIES

Bonnie Loch
O' Aiberdeen,
Biggit ower
Wi' Granite stane!

Biggit ower
But an' ben,
Fae Kingsland Place
T' Crooked Lane!

Biggit ower
For gweed or ill,
Fae Gallow Gate
T' Woolman Hill.

Biggit ower
In a' but name.
Happit up
Wi' hoose and hame.

Weesht! Hark!
Bairnies' feet
Treetlin ben
John Street.

Whase bairnies
Micht they be?
Lochland bairnies!
Come and see,

Elfin faces,
Twinklin een,
Like the starnies
O' yestreen,

In the bonnie
loch that lay
Ayont Black Freers
Mony a day,

When Wee Folks danced
Their Magic Spell
Upon the Play Green,
Near the Well,

Or speelin up
The Woolman Hill
Wi' fite Maw's feeder
And grey goose quill,

Gaed hipperty hopperty
Doon the Steps
In sarkets green
And velvet keps,

. To cweel their taes
In the water clear,
Fleggin the wits
O' John the Freer

Warslin doon
Fae Black Freers Manse
To catch a trootie
By grace or chance:

Syne hipperty Skipperty
Up Scoole Hill
For a Pixy Jig
In the Grammar Skweel,

Or to play tick- an'- tack
Roon the kirkyard stanes
Wi' Ghaist Raw ghosties
In their teens,

Till Auld St. Nicholas
Cou'dna sleep
Though he coontit hunners
O' black-faced sheep:

And past the vennel
And Wyndmill Hill,
Through Gallow Gate Port
Wi' right gweed will,

Roon Leper's Croft
Like a flaucht O' fire,
To Cunninghar Holes
And Futtiesmyre,

And lipperty lapperty
Ower the links,
To Futty Kirk
In Forty Rig,

Or clickerty Clackerty
Ower Thieves Brig,
By Bowack Croft
And Penny Rig,

Through Justice Port
Or Futties Wynd,
The Castlehill
Was left behind,

And Mercat Cross
And Castlegate-
Crickity crick,
'Twas gettin late.

Picherty Pecherty
Up the Hill,
Past the Chapel
And Friar Will

As he coontit his beads
Wi' a side-long glance,
Or lay a-snorin
In Trinity Manse,

To Carmelite Place
And alang the Green
Whaur Bruce and the Lion
Rode yestreen,

Across Bow Brigg,
Up Windmill Brae,
To the Lang stan'in
This mony a day,

and helterty skelterty
Ower the rig
O'Corby Heugh
In a whirligig,

And hip hooray.
Ower Burn and Denn.
Hark. A horn.
Puff. They're gane.

GRANITE CITY STREETS

THE SILVER CITY was built by strong-hard men, whose beards froze in the winter. A two hundred-weight block was an easy lift to a wall. Young apprentice lads were told "lift it on yer knees first laddie, and the rest is easy".

Chapel Street by gaslight.

ALBERT STREET

From Waverley Place to Whitehall Place

NAMED AFTER QUEEN VICTORIA'S HUSBAND. Archibald Simpson's single and two-storey terraces have a quiet repose about them, and lead up to the United Free Church, which was opened in 1882. The architect R. G. Wilson designed it to be the cathedral for the United Presbyterian denomination, and it looks the part when viewed from the wooded howe of the Denburn.

The other side of the Denburn Brig, at number 52, is "The North East Folklore Collection", an independent source for visitors interested to learn about Aberdeen's own heritage of old.

The balladry of North East Scotland has long been obscured, but just as mica sparkles when the sun shines on granite, Stanley Robertson believes that an international public will gain a deeper love and insight for this quasi-operatic music.

Melville Kirk, 1882.
"The Old Road" to Maidencraig ran through "The Carden Wids"; now you can't see the wood for the spires.

ALBERT TERRACE
From Waverley Place to Carden Place

HIGH MINDED THE WEST END of Aberdeen may be, but nurse-maids fondly referred to landmarks. They were sure to point out "The Tartan Kirkie" to their young charges.

ALBYN PLACE
From Alford Place to Queen's Cross

WHERE GIRLS IN SERVICE rolled up their curls in paper, so that they could look demure in their straight-laced bonnets. Mrs Elmslie's Female Orphan Asylum sent forty-six girls between the ages of four and sixteen to Kirk on Sundays; during the week their education was completed: Aberdeen Society women in the 1860's chose hats from Paris, silk from China, lace from Switzerland and wore superfine stockings that could be drawn through a finger ring. All these had to be properly maintained for the lady of the house.

John Bridgeford Pirie, and the Master Mason John Morgan, were the creators of Queen's Cross Church, which embellishes Aberdeen's own boulevard. Ever since 1881, the granite trade have marvelled at the three contrasting shapes of the tower and spire. There were rival claims for another building nearby, the Orphans' Asylum by Archibald Simpson, often regarded as the finest and most simple granite building in the world.

ALFORD PLACE
From Union Place (Union Street) to Albyn Place

THE ROAD TO THE HIGHLANDS, and farmers stopped at Ba'bie Law's grocer's shop, where there was a good dram at the ready after a busy market day. Next door, the Freekirk College is now known as Ba'bie Law by older residents, and Union Street itself is sometimes referred to as being "frae Castlegate to Ba'bie Law".

ANDERSON DRIVE

ABERDEEN'S RING ROAD – named after Sir Alexander Anderson, Lord Provost of Aberdeen, 1859-1866. He was associated with many business ventures which have subsequently brought prosperity. Under his management, the city was extended over the lands of Rubislaw, Fountainhall and Morningfield.

BON ACCORD
by Mary Brooksbank

I've stood upon The Broadhill,
looked ower the grey North Sea;
turned my een oot ower The Links,
a vision fair sat She,
shimmering in the simmer's sun –
Queen o' The North sae braw.
Beloved by every queyn an' loon,
Aiberdeen awa'.

High upon "The Grampians"
the win's blaw sweet an' free;
tang o' the sea fae Girdleness
like incense wafts tae me.
Marischal's spires high ower the toon,
like sentinals guarding a';
O' Scotland's cities, fairest Queen
is Aiberdeen awa.

The discriminating owners and 👉 architects responsible for bringing the "Newtown" of Aberdeen into being were highly intellectual men; respected friends of Sir Walter Scott and other leading members of Edinburgh Society.

👉 "Old Holburn junction", and Alford Place, named after the Donside village. Ba'bie Law's shop was actually up stone steps in Wellington Place. It was said that "her word was her bond, for she niffer't nae less; shoppie weel stocket, door seldom locket".

Provost Anderson, photographed by 👉 George Washington Wilson. The strained look of the sitter is due to the forceful expression (equivalent to dignity in Victorian eyes) that was adopted during the time of exposure.
In this respect Sir William Reid's informal oil painting of him in the "Dead Members' Gallery" at the Hall of The Incorporated Trades, makes an interesting comparison.

👉 Kennerty's milkmen and horses, Albert Street.

Nae a single grave-steen in St. Nicholas Kirkyard,
Hap it gentle or simple, Provost, Preacher or Bard,
But he'll tell you the story o' wha lies beneath,
Whar he first saw the licht; whar he drew his last breath;
What he did; what he left; was there Love in his heart;
Did he help the down-trodden and play a man's part:
If he did, then be sure his life record will glow
Like a glint of sweet sunshine, through Saunders Munro.

An excerpt from "A Toon Hoose Sketch" by W. Carnie.

BAKER STREET

From South Mount Street to Skene Square

THE WORK OF the Baker Incorporation back in the 1860's. Garrets look out over the rooftops to Italianate Kirk campaniles. Bairns thought that the kirks looked like schools.

BALTIC STREET

Prince Regent Street to the Links

A NAME DATING from the trading days of the Prince Regent, when North East Ports handled large amounts of timber from the Baltic Lands. The timber yards remain, but not places like "the Jungle", which had a language and lore in its own right.

BELMONT STREET

From Union Street to Schoolhill

ONE OF THE FIRST "Granite City Streets" to be built (1774); it retains an air of refinement, and a mingle of mystery. For schoolboys there were the attractions of small shop windows, where catapults, and a large selection of penknives could be seen. The newsagent did a brisk trade in foreign stamps with them.

To picture-goers, "The Flechie Belmont" is now part of cinema folklore.

The Gothic kirks, so much a feature of "The Denburn Precipice", are simply referred to as, "The Backs of Belmont" – somewhere behind the street facade, ceremonial tunes continue to be practised, and reels are danced indoors.

Brooding granite and garrets; small shops line the way to the Art Gallery.

The Co-op Bakery, Berryden Road.
Bairns queued up for hot rolls,
innocently chanting the wartime ditty:

"I knocked on the door,
I asked fir some breid,
the lady she said boom boom,
the baker is deid."

BERRYDEN ROAD
Hutcheon Street to Ashgrove Road

BERRYDEN ROAD ran alongside farm-land within living memory. There was always an audience of city children, eager to learn about harness, watching the Clydesdales' plough. The convoy of milkcarts from the Millbank depot was also an impressive sight. "The Co-opie" commemorated the day of the horse with a weathervane.

BLACK'S BUILDINGS
From Woolmanhill to Spa Street

HAMPERS CONTAINING theatrical costumes were frequently seen here at "Schoolhill" Railway Station. The privately run wardrobes were conveniently situated for the back door of the theatre inside "The Buildings" themselves.

Folk were fond of the old place which shook as the trains rumbled in the railway tunnel. A momentary glimpse of this part of the soot begrimed Denburn valley was all that excited suburban commuters saw, as they were hurled towards the cuttings and Kitty Brewster. Banal "Britain in Bloom" has come to this part of the city. Now it is as if Black's Buildings never existed — only a faded out advertisement for a workers' tea room remains painted on the stone parapet.

BLACKFRIARS STREET
From Woolmanhill to St. Andrew Street

WHERE THE War Memorial Lion looks pleased, and doesn't need feeding. (outsiders can draw their own conclusions.)

In outward appearance "The Triple Kirks" nearby, look like a derelict friary. Blackfriars itself stood in the grounds of Robert Gordon's Hospital.

Children watched country folk boarding the "swallow" buses at bedtime, and started to count all the domes of "Aberdeen's Augustan Age", as they tried to go to sleep above the din. The Rosemount domes include Woolmanhill Hospital, the Cowdray Hall, Central School, and those of "education salvation and damnation" on the Viaduct. Once upon a time, genteel folk put brass knockers on their front doors here, but Blackfriars Street was more recently renowned for the workshops of craftsmen like "Joiner Rae" and "Shoemaker Tulloch".

Blackfriars Street being demolished c.1916 to make way for the war memorial and Cowdray Hall.

23rd August, 1902. The opening of the Gordon Highlanders Institute.

The Gordons (C company) at the Drill Hall 1915. Notice the apron worn over the kilt.

BON-ACCORD CRESCENT

From Bon-Accord Terrace to Old Mill Road

TRAVELLERS APPROACHING Aberdeen by stage-coach caught their first glimpse of "The Granite City" from Holburn Street the great road south to the Brig O'Dee. Bon-Accord Crescent is a commanding prospect set as it is on these heights overlooking the Vale of the Howeburn, and would have impressed any gentleman completing a six-day journey from London. Some folk thought that the Crescent looked like the Hanging Gardens of Babylon.

The mailguard lodged in the cottages at Bon-Accord Crescent alongside the toffs, who had a Windmill Brae man, John England, a black-smith, make them the fine railings of "malleable iron" which remain to this day outside their former homes. This was a street that was proud of the fact that he gave deaf and dumb children a chance in life by teaching them all he knew, without expecting the "keys of the toun". Then, as now, professional men welcome newcomers, considering the fact that if they "brocht a copper into the toun, it wid be a'recht."

> Its impressive curve is a triumph of urban design by Archibald Simpson, who was backed by the Tailor Craft.

BON ACCORD
by Sir William Geddes

Gae name ilk toun, the four seas roun',
There's ane that bears the gree,
For routh o' mense an' grip o' sense—
It lies 'tween Don and Dee.

The Braif Toun, the Aul' Croun,
Time-battered though they be,
We'll cowe the loon, wad pluck them doun,
An' lan' him on the lea, lads,
We'll lan' him on the lea.

BON-ACCORD SQUARE

From East and West Craibstone Streets

AT MEWS COTTAGES, coachmen lived over the dimly-lit harness rooms. The glossy horses, proudly known as "Blue Blacks" were kept in readiness for late night calls. Coach houses are still a feature of "The New Town". Stable hands sat up late, making up dye, blacking and harness polish. The latter was a concoction of "Black Beauty" boot polish, powdered resin and ordinary wax melted by the heat of a carriage lamp. When the day of the motor carriage dawned, private coachmen feared for their jobs, pointing out that "ye canna' pit smoke an' ile on a garden".

"The Muckle Stane o' Bon-Accord".

Outsiders who mistakenly took a short cut through "The Square", were frowned upon, because crinolined ladies "took the air" in the private garden; and by an open window in East Craibstone Street, Archibald Simpson, best remembered architect of "The Granite City" played airs on his violin.

Sadly, there were no fountains in the square, but Alexander MacDonald, a granite merchant, who stayed here, did supply them for Trafalgar Square.

BON-ACCORD STREET

From Union Street to Forthill Road

WHERE THE POST MASTER lived over the stableyard, which he shared with a saddler and carriage builder. A car showroom has taken over from the horses.

Bon-Accord Street, may not have been as gracious as the neighbouring Crescent, but it is still polite.

BRIDGE STREET

From Union Street to Guild Street

WHERE THE ECHOES of the tracer horses and their heavy loads are no longer heard reverberated by these bland buildings. Up eight flights of stairs hidden behind the chiselled granite cliff face, Ching Ling Foo, the silent Chinese (Manchunian), illusionist sipped tea out of a broken saucer. At the top of Bridge Street, the public buildings of the city may still jump out at the unsuspecting, yet already impressed visitor, who has caught a first glimpse of the city on arriving at the railway station. It may be this experience that prompted Thomas Hardy, an outsider to write a poem when honoured by Aberdeen University:

I looked and thought,
"all is too grey and cold
to wake my place enthusiasms of old,"
till a voice passed
"behind that granite mein
lurks the imposing beauty of a Queen."

I looked anew
and saw the radiant form of Her
who soothes in stress who steers in storm, of
the grave influence of those eyes sublime
men count for the stability of time.

Bridge Street, and Bridge Street Stairs. A bet was won by a man who climbed up the latter on his hands.

Bairns spying on courting couples would chant:

"first he gave me an aipple
then he gave me a pear,
then he gave me 'a tanner'
to kiss me on The Stair."

Bridge Street is carried on arches, and where tall buildings now stand on the West side of the street was a wooden stairway, running down in front of these boarded-up arches. On the open ground of Bridge Place there stood a circus tent made of wood, with a canvas roof. A young equestrienne used to twinkle down the steps of a nearby caravan, wearing tights, a short skirt and spangles for her nightly performance. John Bell amazed Aberdonians by making good mahogany furniture from the old dock gates; but even this achievement must pale beside the spectacular circus displays, which included the taking of Rorke's Drift, Dick Turpin's ride to York and the carnival on ice, with displays of roller-skating on a boarded floor. James Leatham also minded on Marshall's moving panorama and diorama, which showed views of Edinburgh and the Shrine of the Holy Nativity at Bethlehem, in 1842.

BROADFORD
Otherwise Maberly Street
From George Street to Rosemount Place and Skene Square

"DA' SAYS YE MECHT hae sair han's at Broadfords, but its better than hain' weet, cail feet at 'The Fish'."

Lassies used to chap at their friend's windows on their way to work at the mill, shouting maybe for Maggie to "hurry up and never mind yer steys – grab yer rowie it's the Quarter".

The Menfolk were woken from their slumbers when the Broadford Bell rang; their wives adding "rise tae yer work John, its me fa speaks tae ye – dinnae think ye are biding with yer aul' wife noo – Rise tae yer work John, for yer nae feeling weel – pit yer workin' jacket on – Here gings the factory bell".

It was an old saying amongst working men who intended getting married that it was a case of "Spring Garden for Poverty,
The Wool Mill for pride –
The Boag Mill for a bonnie lass;
and Broadford for a bride".

BROAD STREET
From Union Street to Gallowgate

"IT'S NAE AS BIG as the pyramids, but it looks better" – The race of builders who erected the four hundred foot long granite west front of Marischal College, allowed themselves some self satisfaction, after they had sat up late at night figuring out a practical solution to problems that maybe the architect hadn't foreseen. They were probably the best in the world at their trade, and could confidently tell the Aberdeen Architect Sir Ninian Cowper, "you draw the Seabury Memorial Cathedral, and we'll build it" – The Wall Street Crash dashed the prospects of there being "a City Square" opposite Marischal College, which would have featured the cathedral (whose spire was to have replaced that of St. Nicholas Kirk, which was lost to the city skyline in 1874), as well as Provost Skene's House.

On the proposed site for the cathedral stands a simple tower block of offices ironically called St. Nicholas House. Marischal College was floodlit by gas, from the very day it opened.

Dawvid Glibetongue's Harangue
by James Ogg

"For honest workmen, sharp and keen,
I rede you gang to Aberdeen.
Our sons are famed for manly graces,
our daughters too for dandie dresses;
our local buiks for charmin' readin',
our farmers, bricks for cattle breedin'.
for a' that's noble, grand and jeety,
I point you to "The Granite City",
We're famed for a' that's great an' gweed,
aye, e'en for makin' potted heid.
In ither cities I hae seen
"fine potted heid fae Aberdeen."

 John Bell cabinet maker "antique and broken furniture renovated and made perfect. Work carefully done, charges moderate".

BROADFORDS *by W. Cadenhead (1898).*

O, Mary, lass, I'm glad again
Tae see you at yer loom;
Yer e'e will noo get back its glance,
Yer cheek its wonted bloom.
It wis a waesome thocht, eneugh
The hert wi' grief to fill,
The stoppin' o' the throng an' stir
O' busy Broadford Mill.

The stately engines move again,
Ance mair the spindles hum;
There's music in the very belt
That whirls aroon' the drum;
The shuttle whistles through the warp
A liltie blythe an' gay,
An' like the beating o' a hert's
The lappin' o' the lay.

The very bairnies loup wi' joy
Tae see the reekin' lums;
They ken that Da' gets wage again
Fan e'er Thursday comes:
The bassie's fu' o' meal ance mair,
There's bannocks on the board;
An' mingling wi' the nightly thanks
Comes "Blessings on Broadford".

An' simmer evenin's sweet,
Fin oot amang the trees an' flow'rs
The lads an' lasses meet;
An' fan the week comes near the end,
A sigh for rest I draw—
But wageless, unsought idleseat—
Gweed keep it frae us a'!

Then let us hail the factory din
Again wi' cheery smile,
An' bless the bell wha's welcome soond
Invites us tae oor toil:
Lang may we timely thrang the gates,
Wi' grateful hert an' will,
At gathering an' at lowsin' hour—
O' guid auld Broadford Mill.

Broadfords' Horses hauled great bales
of jute at the Brick Mill in Maberly
Street.

"The biggest banquet that Scotland ever saw" was held in a marquee erected by Lord Strathcona on the east side of The Gallowgate. A replica of one of the city gates was built at the top of Broad Street, and 2,500 of Strathcona's guests filed into dinner at a cost of £9,000. The great west front of Marischal College has been stencilled onto commemorative china plaques, and even described as "Wedding Cake" architecture. It seems that everything other than rich cake was on the menu after the opening ceremony in September 1906.

"The polished pinnacles and frosty spires" of Marischal College.

CITY OF GRANITE TOWER
by Ronald Campbell MacFie

City of granite tower and granite spire,
Of grim, indomitable granite will,
Deep in your granite heart the cosmic fire
Is burning still . . .

Epigram of Dr. Arthur Johstoun, Physician-
in-ordinary to King Charles I, upon the City
of Aberdeen – translated by Rev. John
Barclay, Minister of Cruden.

Whoe'er thou art, that Rome dost magnifie,
And her extol as people fondly do,
Entitling her the Earth's delight and Queen,
Compare with he the City ABERDEEN,
A city which doth neighbour with the sea,
To which the ocean waves do constantlie
Flow up as handmaids, yet ere they approach
They stoop as fearing too far to encroach.
From lofty hills both cities view with pryd,
Both from their stately and their thundering
    tower
Defye with threatenings all unfriendly power,
Rome of her Tabii and unconqueered host
Of Scipios and of great Caesars boasts.
This city of her Menzeises great worth,
Of Cullens and of Lawsons here brought
    forth,
And Collisons, all men of great esteem;
Of these she boasts, these doth her glory
    deem.
If bigness may 'mongst praises reck'ned be
Rome is indeed of greater bulk than she—
But in all Gifts and Ornaments of mind
Rome may her Equals in this find.

"Building a church, is an act of
worship", wrote the architect of
Aberdeen's Seabury Memorial
Cathedral, which was to have stood in
Broad Street.

Marischal College seen from the
granite spire of St. Nicholas Kirk,
1906. Builders' ladders are still in
evidence scaling the facade.

75

CANAL ROAD

From Causewayend to the Canal Bridge

THIS WAS THE packman's track to old Aberdeen; a resting and watering place for horses. An encampment where the fires were always burning; and many a fine air was heard on the bagpipes and fiddle.

It is no wonder then, that this meeting place brought forth such a talent as Jeannie Robertson, M.B.E., a housewife, whose incomparable voice, in addition to the art of projecting the ancient balladry of her lineage, first captivated audiences saddened by the loss of Kathleen Ferrier from the concert platform in 1953.

Jeannie's cousin, Gordon Robertson (Royal Scots, now of Sydney) found different words than the public tributes, when he wrote this coronach:

"She raised the wolves of Donnachaidh
from nadir to the zenith —
well endowed with Burns' muse,
scion of Celtic Kenneth (MacAlpine Mor)
the Covenanters' sagas sang,
of battles midst the broom;
Virtutis Gloria Merces Domine,
commendo Jeannie's spiritum."

Cockie Hunter's Bargain Store, Castle Terrace.

CASTLE TERRACE

From Castle Street to Canal Terrace

THE ORIGINAL CASTLE was destroyed by the Bruce party in 1308; what remains is in fact a Cromwellian bastion. A prominent feature on old engravings was the beacon at St. Ninian's chapel on Castlehill. This building passed through a number of vicissitudes as a mortuary, a quakers' prison in the 1660's, when it was recorded that prisoners couldn't see their own food without the help of a candle, besides being blown up by the Jacobites. In 1794, the Duke of Gordon, who is commemorated in Roman fashion with toga, laid the foundation stone of the barracks. The military hospital, on the adjoining Heading Hill, followed in 1799.

Castle Terrace is remembered for the Sick Children's Hospital, with its balconies, that made it look like a galleon at sea.

CAUSEWAYEND

From Gallowgate to Powis Place

A LEAN STREET, where many children died in the depression years.

Poets have written about the slaty greyness of the Powis Place district, and the cutting weather there on November nights. This was a place where even young women wore dark shawls. Their little houses have been swept away, although a meeting place, known as "The Coffiny" with its summer seat remains temporarily as a reminder of the old days.

The stark silhouette of "The Balmoral Tower" at Causewayend School is a motorway landmark on the inner city link road, which is beginning to be flanked by oil company offices. Can love or gold change Causewayend for ever, now that Bendelow's Pie shop has gone?

CHARLOTTE STREET

From St. Andrews Street to Maberley Street

QUEEN CHARLOTTE WAS respected by Aberdeen. This street runs the complete length of the former loch, and bears her name, but folk knew the place better as being the home of Mutter Howey, railway contractor. Carters competed for the best turn out, and well groomed horses that liked "butter bars", stood twenty hands high. Matched pairs of hearse horses were stabled here, making daily trips to "where they were required".

CHERRYBANK

COTTAGES AT 52 Bon-Accord Terrace.

CIRCUM BENDIBUS

A RAILWAY LINE which was to have run from Woodside, via Stockethill, Queen's Cross and Albyn Place to Guild Street.

COLLEGE STREET AND SOUTH COLLEGE STREET

DOMINATED BY the railway arches. The first viaduct was constructed of brick in 1848, but was replaced with granite in 1904.

Under the arches, family businesses established themselves, and brewery drays set out from here to deliver Black's beer from Devanha Brewery to local bars.

COMMERCE STREET

From Regent Quay to Justice Street, East North Street and Park Street

CONSTRUCTED IN 1760, as part of "The Shorelands Improvement".

A cast iron bridge linked the Barracks to their hospital.

Cockie Hunter's store was "itself a hub of Commerce". The family prided themselves on selling anything from a needle to an anchor.

> "If ye want a knocker for your door
> or a hoose tae fit yer fleer.
> Ging tae Cocky Hunter's Store in
> Aiberdeen".

CONSTITUTION STREET

From "The Park Road, across the Aberdeenshire Canal to the Links"

BUILT IN 1807 as "Park Place", over "Fill the Cap Croft", at the north side of the Castlehill. Writing about buildings and decay isn't the stuff of life – so this is not an epitaph – St. Peter's catholic school (now the Shiprow Tavern) is a reminder of the large families who were crowded into this quarter of the city.

 Commerce Street.

Trams came this way to the beach. Horses were stabled at the tram-shed, and railway bank plotties benefited from the manure. The Constitution Street granite yard of MacDonald that sculpted "The Granite Duke", delivered him to the Castlegate; and the team of horses that obliged, were thought to be worthy of mention here, by unofficial historians.

COTTON STREET
From Miller Street to Links Road

WHERE SALMON WORKERS and weatherbeaten men who took their stallions around the farms in the summer, found work in the winter. Gas works wages were not high, because there was plenty of labour to be found elsewhere.

Cotton Street was home for railway guards and foremen who worked at Waterloo Station. Schoolchildren who used the playing field on the links thought that the shoppie here sold the finest penny drinks. On the way back to Hanover Street and more lessons, they marvelled at the heavy men and heavy horses of the Shoreporters workforce. Bairns came down here with prams to buy coal and cinders, but found a few that had fallen out of the gasworks engine cab: "Paddy at the railway picking up steens — along came an engine and knocked Paddy's beens. 'Oh', said Paddy, 'that's na fair', 'Oh', said the engine man, ye shouldnae be there'."

🚂 Gas Works Engine.

CRAIBSTONES STREET
From Bon-Accord Street to Bon Accord-Crescent

JOHN CRAB'S LAND. A march stone commemorates the massacre of 1644.

Co-op Bakery and Meal Mill.

CRAIGIE LOANINGS, ROSEMOUNT

From Albert Street and Whitehall Place to Rosemount Place

A LANE named after a fifteenth century burgess, Alexander Crag. With Aberdeen's penchant for the diminutive, the mannie's lands became known as Craggie Loanings and Crag became Craig.

CROOKED LANE

From St. Andrew Street to Loch Street

L AID OUT on the banks of the former Loch. Carters and coal dealers had their stores here. The Oddfellows, a small bar here only accommodated a few folk, including boys who took lemonade. "The toilet only held half a man".

Cinder wives from Cotton Street.

 "Indian Baroque" in Bridge Street.

Masonic Temple, Crown Street. 👉

CROWN STREET
From Union Street to Ferryhill Road

ALTHOUGH THIS IS ONE of the oldest Granite City streets, (it was all built by 1828), the chief architectural glories came much later. Instead of Crown Place, there stands a tower house castle (The Post Office). The Masonic Temple is unique and awe inspiring. It has the hallmark of a James Gibbs design. It is one of the city's celebrated understatements that the emminent architect was "a Fittie loon forgotten". The portrait studio used by the photographer George Washington Wilson, made way for an imposing office building, in which the Etching King James McBey had a small studio before he left Aberdeen. The "Star and Garter" building is tall, so the Windmillbrae is the best vantage point to see how this corner embellishes Crown Street, and gives the place an air of importance.

Crown Street, looking towards Golden Square from Crown Place c. 1900. The cabbies wait at their stance by the Music Hall, (c. 1900).

James Cassie (left), John Philip "of Spain" (centre), and fellow artist.

Cassie claimed Aberdeen should be regarded as the cradle of Scottish art. He said, "There's Jamesone, Dyce, and Philip; tak' awa' Aberdeen an' twal' mile roun an fa' are ye?" George Washington Wilson himself was an artist before he made photography his profession. He exported his stereoscopic views and lantern slides to far away places like Shanghai. His North East personalities 1852-56 were a collotype collage portrait gallery of leading citizens who were thought to be "far better than a walk in the churchyard, more expressive than a funeral sermon".

The Social Chess Club came to the Crown Street Portrait Studio on May 11th 1861 "to hae their photies teen". George Walker was a friend of the photographer, and they both joked as the members attempted to look studious. To start with, clouds of smoke from church-warden pipes concealed the field of battle, and the Rev. Keay (centre right back row) "loomed through like an East Indiaman in a heavy fog!"

Back row
Alexander Martin, teacher at the Grammar School;
later rector. Reverend Robert Gray, maths master,
Towns Schools, Little Belmont Street. Reverend
William Keay, Woodside Parish. George Walker,
bookseller of A. Brown & Co., author of "Aberdeen
Awa'." Charles MacDonald, teacher at the Grammar
School.

Front row
Robert Alexander, teacher, Towns Schools. Dr. John
Brebner, Grammar School. Reverend William
Barrack, rector, Grammar School. Reverend Dr.
James Fraser, St. Clements. Reverend Alex. Beverley,
Latinist, Grammar School. William Forsyth, editor
"Aberdeen Journal".

Crown Street and Crown Place, 1900. The Post Office building now occupies the site of the gardens.

DEE STREET

From Union Street to Dee Place

THIS ORIGINALLY WAS "Upper Dee Street." "Lower Dee Street," nearer the Denburn, was an older thoroughfare.

Upper Dee Street still resembles a row of granite dolls' houses, with pretty gardens, straight out of a bairn's story book.

The Jewish Synagogue stands mute, in a terrace. The Aberdeen Jews are buried at "The Grove."

☞ 43 Dee Street.

DEE VILLAGE SQUARE

A PLANNED COURTYARD VILLAGE, built of local brick, and had the pleasant feature of the Ferryhill burn running through the grounds.

This was a fine backie, in which bairns could play, and a rare place for impromptu parties: "There's a party in the backie, won't ye come won't ye come — bring yer ane farthing biscuit, an' yer ane penny bun!"

The old men sat around, and watched the young women on washday whose boast it was that "I can wash a sailor's sark, and I can wash it cleano; I can wash a sailor's sark and bleach it on yon greeno."

The Hydro Electric Board offices were built over the lassies' drying place, and the very roofs of Dee Village, with its pantiles made at neighbouring Clay hills, have ceased to be a feature of Crown Street "for mony a year."

☞ Dee Village, 1898.

DEVANHA TERRACE

From South Crown Street to Prospect Terrace

AN IMPRESSIVE terrace overlooks the Dee (this is the Roman version of the name).

Aberdeen's only two storey "but and ben" is a rural reminder of the Deeside Railway, built in 1853 and closed, 1966.

DEVANA

It has been inferred by many "unofficial historians" that "Devana" was the forerunner of Aberdeen, because the settlement occupied a commanding position on the left bank of the Diva, (Dee); and the inhabitants, along with six tribes led by Galgacus, were defeated in 84 AD.

The street name Caledonian Place indicates the approximate position where the Caledonians watched the advance of the Roman legions upon "Devana".

Today the Roman and his trouble lie ashes under "Conservation Area Number Five", which includes Archibald Simpson's "Devanha House", which appropriately enough does look Roman.

☞ Wellington Bridge, gateway to Devana.

☞ Devanha House, dated 1840.

DRUM'S LANE
From Upperkirkgate to Loch Street

AT ONE TIME, this was the secluded garden ground where widows and spinster residents of Lady Drum's Hospital strolled at leisure.

When Drum's Lane had a school, this narrow lane didn't seem so melancholy. This version of an old street song still brings back a cheerful echo.

"Doon in Drum's Lane there lives a Chinese woman. If ye want a kiss ye have tae pay a shilling; soldiers half-a-crown, sailors half-a-guinea, working men, five pound ten, children only a penny."

ELMBANK

RATHER SELECT VILLAS were built along the bank of the Aberdeenshire canal. The dark thickets of the Powis Estate, with its secluded mansion house on the distant ridge, and the pool of fishes after which it was named, made this, in comparison, the sunnyside.

At 16 Elmbank Road, the composer Ronald Center was born on 2nd April, 1913. His compositions are now more often performed outside Aberdeen. Fervid and throbbing, the message he conveys, hints at the depths of North East consciousness.

Bathing Stations, Sea Beach. 🖛

ESPLANADE, SEA BEACH

From North Pier to Bathing Station

IN GLASGOW FAIR WEEK the crowd sang on the sands. Buskers tap danced on ribbed mats; ice-cream "sliders" were sold, and at Madame Veitch's light pink and blue caravan, palms were read and the mysteries of the crystal ball interpreted. Mack's telescope gave a halfpenny gaze at "the boaties comin' in", and the children who stood at the point of the North Pier fishing for mackerel could be clearly seen.

The silhouette of the "Siberian" seawater bathing station with its "Russian Bath" overlooked the bathing machines which the Aberdeen Police and Waterworks Act protected by sentencing offenders under the age of fourteen to twelve lashes with the tawse by the official whipper.

Crowds from the open decked trams made their way past the beachballs in hanging nets and the wooden handled red tin spades, and paused at the shop to buy macaroon cakes.

Sea Beach *With the Seasons Greetings* Aberdeen

By the sands, the "original" pierots performed, and at the punch and judy shows there was also slight of hand.

"Professor" Powsie set himself alight when he splashed into a round shallow tank of water from a high scaffold, and on occasions there were balloon ascents.

From the Broadhill, children watched practice runs with the lifeboat, and the salmon coble boat at work. From "The Misers' Hillie" a view of the Pittodrie football ground could be obtained. The narrow lane to the Trinity cemetery was haunted by "The Green Lady", but this didn't distract the gamblers, courting couples, or "Twang", a worthy who slept there wrapped up in newspaper.

Behind the allotments that supported prize roses, rhubarb and hens, children washed their faces in the dew on the first of May.

Duckworth's Pond was popular for sailing boats. On the pony rides, one year olds had their first experience of horsemanship, whilst their parents held them grimly on. Fathers could test their skill by boxing three rounds for a pound against a professional at "the Booths", to the background accompaniment of The Gordons' brass band.

Excitement for the workers was provided by the early aeroplane spins. For the less wealthy, the scenic railway got them off the ground.

G. S. Fraser wrote fondly of "The Gas Works, the White Ballroom and the red brick baths and salmon nets along a mile of shore."

FISH STREET

From "The Tarry Brig" to Albion Street

THE MASONS who built the world famous Gothic cathedrals of Europe would not have been ashamed of the craftsmanship of West St. Clement's church. Their masterpieces will be admired for ever, but West St. Clement's is gone. A notice proclaimed these facts to the last: "Sunday school by the side door: Lifeboys, Monday at seven, minister's interview; Thursday evening, Boys' Brigade, Friday at 7.30, choir at 8 pm.

 Fish Street; West St. Clement's Church. A vanished landmark by "The Tarry Briggie".

FISHER SQUARES FOOTDEE

ALONE BY THE dunes with the distant neighing of horses on the Queen's Links, before the Gasworks and seabathing station were built there was a smell of boilyards and boatbuilding. Incoming vessels might see a cow from the Shetland boat escape on arrival at Findlay's Buildings, and make for the north breakwater with chiels and drovers in pursuit, past "Scartie's Monument," a sewer vent. On "The Back Links," kitchen furniture was scrubbed down with sand on washday, when sheets were bleached, and clothes dried along the shore.

Women sat on the seat by the Gent's "Yettie," wearing new wraps, white aprons and blue petticoats, and remarked about family likenesses during "a Launchin'," when everbody got into the shipyards. Men who worked in the heat of the hulls at Hall's, went home at night through the arch to Neptune Terrace, with their moleskins and linders so wet that they had to be left on the brass rail in front of the fire. On Fridays, the ganger was paid for piecework, and the money distributed in the Neptune Bar.

When "The Fittie Picnic" passed by to Culter, headed by the Oakbank pipeband playing "Saviour like a shepherd lead us," it seemed unlikely that these people, so fiercely

 North Square, FootDee.

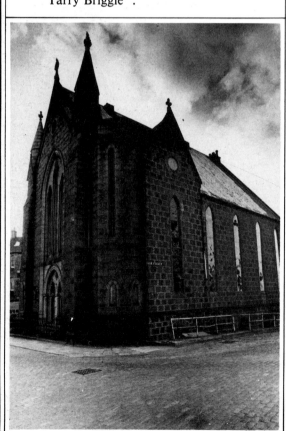

proud of their girls, could yell "steen him oot Jock, he's a toonser."

Before breakfast, women shelled mussels or baited, and might walk in search for the latter as far as "The Black Dog". Children who were late risers work to the chastisement of "Fat's keepin' ye, ye lazy quine, it's been a rare forenee". The clink as regular as clockwork, of empty mussel shells hitting the base of the tub, and ring of hammers at Davidson's cooperage, or the creak from Duthie's ropeworks, were all early morning sounds before school "went in".

◾ Cast iron "wallee", "Fittie".

On Fridays, sandboys with their donkeys delivered fresh smelling seasand for the floors.

Despite hard work, and up in the morning to "Teem breeks and gapin' leather", many fishermen were unable to raise the money to buy their cottages. "Fittie men" were well known as skippers with the herring fleet from Stornoway down to Yarmouth. At night, by the light of oily lamps the wives made nets to "catch the silver darlings".

If boats were in distress when "crossing the bar", women tore their hair an clapped their hands; their piercing cries and frantic gestures couldn't be forgotten. A bust on the parapets of the pilot's office commemorates the wreck of a barque, the *Grace Darling,* lost offshore on 27th February, 1874. Drink aboard the doomed vessel was significant, and there are no longer any public houses in the Squares, or on Pocra Quay, where men had their "wacht o' ale" and lounged at the gable ends, or played "pitch and toss", keeping warm by a particular sweeping motion of the arms. In the best room set aside for marriages and funerals, the clock on the mantlepiece, "the wag a' th' wa'," silently chimed the hours surrounded by the glazed expressions of framed photographs.

◾ Cattle from Shetland were herded off the boats into a large wooden shed by "The Round House". This distant view of the Fisher Squares shows scaffolding straddling The Breakwater.

Through the house, "the guidwife at hame", welcomed unexpected visitors. "It's sair matter that we're oot o' biskit an' fite breed; but there's ait kyaaks and bannocks t'ee". Usually children were good eaters, having "a crop fir a' corn, and a baggie to hud' it".

◾ Baxter's "tarry wash-hoose".

A FEW ABERDEEN "GIPSIES"
(children's jingles)

"Eat-a-lottle,
black bottle
eat-a-lottle out"
Tak' a dirty dish cloot
and push him right out.

Ippity sippity, ippity sap
ippity sippity, kinella kinapp –
Kinella up, kinella doon
Kinella into China toon.

One two three four five,
a sailor took a dive;
he cut his throat
with a five pound note –
one two three four five

One two three a leerie,
I spy Bella Peerie
sitting on her bumbleerie,
eating chocolate babies.

I am your master
pit-a-patter on your shoulder
pit-a-patter on your shoulder
I am your master.

Caw caw the ropie
my ma's awa tae the shoppie
to buy a cake o' soapie.

Eenie meanie makaraka
rado dominaka
sallamaka ellenaka
rum tum scum scush.

At play in New Pier Road, FootDee.

FREDERICK STREET
From King Street to Park Street

THE FREDERICK STREET public school changed the skyline of this quarter of the city when it opened in 1905. Originally it could take 332 infants and 764 senior/junior pupils. The rooftop playground measured 750 square yards, children skipped to their favourite games like "caw caw the ropie" – when playing with a ball they would sing "one, two, three a leerie, I spied Bella Peerie." Some sang and played "The Grand Old Duke of York", "the farmer in the Dell", "in and out the dusty bluebells" and "ring a ring o' roses".

Frederick Street School's rooftop playground. On the opposite side of the street was Shuttle Lane School, where charity dinners were held in the festive season, when "Mr Ledingham the baker gave 500 lbs of plum pudding for the delectation of waifs".

GEORGE STREET
From St. Nicholas Street to Powis Terrace

THE OLD CENTRE of the manufacturing town, and renowned for saddlesoap weaving and horn combs. Handcarts fairly hurled along, loaded high with wooden bedframes, flock mattresses or household effects from tenement removals. When old people decided to move to a ground floor flat, they left a note stating "I'm flitting fae the top o' the hoose to a low door". Handcart men overtook carters at the "Killing Hoose Corner" traffic lights, Hutcheon Street, and were advised to buy a horse and cart, thus avoiding obstruction. The reponse came readily enough, that if they were as strong as their voice, they wouldn't need a horse to pull the cart.

"The Jolly Boys Drive", organised by the West side Dairy, was a highlight of the year for local children. They sold "Jubilee milk", and won a silver teapot for the best Dairy turn out at the Kittybrewster show.

George Street, 1911. 👈

GERRARD STREET
From Gallowgate to George Street

NAMED AFTER a minister of Greyfriars Kirk who was a professor of theology at the old Marischal College.

Today, the tenements where the Broadford Mill lassies stayed have been replaced by high rise flats "The shoppie with its little entrance bell" where they got their messages in, has gone, leaving the Kirk with its moorish minarets in splendid isolation.

👈 "The Best dairy turn out in Aberdeen" Westside Dairy, 235 George Street.

GOLDEN SQUARE

WHERE DELIVERY BOYS tip-toed down basement stairs to pay their first call at the kitchens of stately granite town houses, carrying hooped baskets covered with a white cloth.

Servants wearing freshly laundered aprons gave them a piece of fruit or shortbread, because housekeepers relied on tradesmen "By Royal Appointment" in their daily planning, to do "impossibilities straight away", even if "miracles might take a little longer." Next it was the turn of the window cleaners who saw that the long sash windows gleamed every day.

A leerie was instructed to light the lamps early on winter afternoons, and set off round the square with his ladders, paraffin, and "take me matches". If passers by pointed out the silhouette of a prosperous man through undraped windows whilst the lantern glass was being cleaned (so that the light shone brightly), he was sure to remark that "it's the wecht o' his watch an' chain that's makin' him bow'd."

The lights cast many a flickering shadow, and today, only "The Granite Duke" remembers the Castlegate ghost stories, as he muses over the siliconed tin of advocates' limousines.

"Below stairs", weatherbeaten bobbies on the evening beat supped strong tea out of bowls in the housekeeper's room and ate her scones, whilst their outsize bicycle saddles soaked up the dew against the railings.

"The Fountain", Woodside.

GREAT NORTHERN ROAD

"THE NEW INVERURIE ROAD TO THE NORTH", from Kittybrewster to Scatterburn, was thronged with carts on Tuesdays and Fridays, with farmers coming to and fro from the Mart.

Tramcars clanged their way backwards and forwards from St. Nicholas Street to Woodside, or alternatively to Scatterburn. Amid the bustling shopping area, there was a much-loved Fountain. The tramcar depot provided a certain amount of interest, and bairns would shout "D-Dictation, Corporation, how many trams are in the station?", and counted them accordingly by bouncing rubber balls. From the top-deck of the tramcar they also counted churches, or maybe looked down at the Haudagains Camping Ground, and wished that they "lived in a caravan, travelling the road like a gypsy-man". Some folk thought that this was a setting for a romantic novel—a nice love-story, without any searing hardships in it, to browse through at the library—but others were wary of "The Travelling People", who were waiting to be rehoused by Aberdeen Corporation.

It was a "weel-kent" saying that "my mither says, I should'na go, doon where the gypsies camp below—if I should, she would say 'naughty, naughty bairn, to disobey' ". Nevertheless, this community thrived well into the 1950s.

UWAY TAY EIBURDEEN

A screen to the blasting screams of the
    North Sea
Lay Aberdeen in wait for me, daring to travel
    north.

On that blessed morn the freeze licked my
    cheeks
'Till, reaching the kirk, unknown friends
    greeted me,
loading my inner body with scones and tea,
    feeding the weary, hungry traveller.

On that very eve sat I by a fire,
Where wee Gabi wound her arms around me
Keeping warm the lonely traveller.

But further north,
Fetterangus greeted my ears with lovely song;
Yea, she sang for me,
    The kind lady,
    The lady wi' the tree
Gladdening me, a waking northern traveller.

Christopher Tucker of Mexico, dedicated this poem to Stanley Robertson and Jane Turriff, thanking them for their hospitality.

"For it's seven lang years since we busked
    together;
the seasons may cheenge, but there's nae
    cheenge in me
For she's gentle and pure as the snaw wreaths
    in winter,
fan they're laid oot tae bleach on the hills o'
    Glenshee."

An excerpt from "The Maid o' Glenshee."

"Tam, Tam the piper's son
learned tae play fan he wis young;
the only tune that he could play
wis "O'er the hills and far away."

Haudagain camp-site, 11th July, 1934. Folk, young or old, who resided here, were brought up with a belief in the old adage that "nobody leaves an Aberdonian's home with an empty belly or a sair hert".

"There wis a jolly beggarman,
and he was dressed in green,
and he was seeking lodgings
at a hoose near Aiberdeen.

I'll gang nae mair a-rovin',
late intae the nicht—
an' I'll gang nae mair a-rovin',
tho' the meenshine nae sae bricht."

(An excerpt from the classical ballad, "The Jolly Beggarman".)

THE ONE-MAN BAND

"I am 'The Music Man'
frae doon yer way,
an' I can play."
"Fit can ye play?"
"The Mouthie.....sook an' blaw.
The cymbals.....clash an' clang.
The drum.....thump an' bump.
The bells.....ting aling."

GREAT WESTERN ROAD

From Nellfield Cemetery to the Waterworks

COVENT GARDEN MARKET Porters thought that Robert Balmanno's plants yielded the finest crop of strawberries in Great Britain, during the 18th Century.

"The 'Manno' field Enclosures" that he farmed as strawberry fields, in the vicinity of present-day Cromwell and Countesswells Roads, must not be confused with those that "The Beatles" immortalised in folk-song.

Names like Friendship Farm and Friendville pre-date "The New Deeside Road". The terraces, with neatly finished bargeboards, terra cotta ridging and gablets, resemble the Balmoral Estate cottages; so tourists feel at home in this "Bed and Breakfast Alley", although young folk on the milk rounds used to give a few houses less respectable tee-names, when cold-shouldered at the Tradesmen's Entrance.

Parcel Boys found that the "Mannofield Run" up to the Tram Depot didn't yield much in the way of penny tips, but they were prepared to help elderly passengers transfer to Wilkie's Suburban Tram that went on to Bieldside, at the terminus.

Some schoolchildren went home to lunch, and in consequence, the wooden floor of the top-deck soon got worn down. Others played in the green loaning, opposite Broomhill School—this ancient track led down to the Cot-Toun of Ruthrieston, from "The Old Deeside Road", and was known as "The Woodies". Couthie-sounding, but unfashionable, Pitmuxton, and the Bleachgreens nearby, are yet remembered by old Travelling-Men, who were invited to play the bagpipes here, around the time of Hogmanay.

"Kelly o' Cults" delivery cairt.

The new street names give an impression that this is the City's French Quarter, with its chic "Villes" and "Places". Even Nellfield has become a "Champs Elysées", with rosebeds adjacent to the shops and Trades' Hall—"Tres Jolie"; but beyond the cemetery wall, which runs "a fair skelp" up the Great Western Road, this Granite City Street leads inexorably on . . . from soaring church steeple to soaring church steeple; from spirelets and Mansard roofs to spirelets and Mansard roofs.

GUILD STREET

From Market Street to Bridge Street

NAMED AFTER THE good Doctor Guild who purchased the monastery of Trinity Friars and gave it to the incorporated trades.

Teenage tracer boys were employed to guide the heavy loads up Marischal, Market and Bridge Streets. They frequented Guild Street when business was slack, making sure that a "mou'-bag" weight dangled from the horse's collar, thus preventing the wooden bottomed canvas from knocking passers-by. A perquisite of the job was the end-product, which sold for a penny a bucket.

The station yard often was the place where new arrivals were photographed; Washington Wilson, whose firm was kept busy recording the new locations of statues as the corporation had them moved to the bewilderment of visitors; gave one of the carillon bells from Louvain, to the Town.

Fiddler's Wallie was presented to "the inhabitants of the world" by Sandy Fiddler, a dealer in coalies by the quay. The watch that was given as a token of appreciation cost £20, and to the amusement of Aberdonians, the well only cost £18.

HENRY STREET

From Skene Street to the boundary wall of "The Bridewell"

PROVOST HENRY, the last man to powder his hair in the old fashioned way, was honoured by having a short street that led up to the ladies' prison, named after him.

Fame was short lived, and Henry has now been joined to Rose Street.

HADDEN STREET

From Market Street to Carmelite Street

NAMED AFTER James Hadden, Lord Provost 1801-1831, known as "The Father of the City" because due to his foresight Union and King streets were laid out; and the improvement to the harbour by Thomas Telford realised.

The family business of Alexander Hadden, whose chimney dominated the south end of The Green, were the first to introduce improved hosiery machinery, by Arkwright. "country loons looking for a fee, a brown paper parcel under their arm, stood in wait looking for employers who wore large gold watch chains. The corn exchange depot was where bargains were struck with a dram, and a slap of the hand."

Horse parades were held here with patent leather and silver buckles. Remarks were overheard "its a lot o' flash, but the tails hae recht tied up."

After the horsedealing was over women were present in and around the bars . . .

At the tram terminus Holburn Street. 🖛 Harry Gordon referred to a fat woman who squeezed into a tramcar on its way to Brig O' Don, during a show at The Beach Pavilion in 1927.

HAMILTON PLACE

From Craigie Loanings to Forest Road

A PUNCHBOWL OF architectural styles ranging from lobbies shaped like horseshoes to spirelet rooms, where families who could afford a telescope trained it on the stars and the neighbours.

The street is named after a professor who built an observatory on the Castlehill. At the west end of Hamilton Place lived an East End worthy, the dancing master Francis Peacock, who eloquently called his country retreat "The Villa Franca." One successful tradesman tried to buy respectability when he built an imposing retirement home in granite; but found that to the toonsfolk he was still "the snuff dealer that bides at Sneezin' Ha'."

HOLBURN STREET

From Union Street to the Brig O' Dee

THE NEW ROAD south over the Howeburn from which it takes its name was a dusty thoroughfare, with glossy country horses often appearing grey before they reached town.

Showpiece saddles and hems were made for ploughing matches at the old saddlers shop beside the Brig O' Dee Bar.

Holborn Street, 🖛 and St. Nicholas Union Grove.

HUNTLY STREET

From Union Street to Rose Street

THE PRIDE OF Huntly Street is the granite crockets of one of Aberdeen's three cathedrals. The soaring spire is regarded as a ladder up to Heaven, when a ray of sunshine makes the mica sparkle.

The rich had to leave their granite mansions behind them, but were sure to be seen off by a crowd of several hundred eager to hear the contents of the will. It was not unusual for twenty Rolls Royce cars to gather for the occasion, falling in with the procession. An expensive mahogany coffin, and bishops in vestments added to the solemnity of the occasion.

At the other end of this "L" shaped street was the West prison, brooding over the blank looking tenements. That building is now ancient history, but one question remains unanswered: Did the nearby ropeworks supply the town's hangman?

Latterly, the Asylum and workshop for blind people has made the street a household name; but John Smith's impressive building which served their needs since 1843 has been made into office accommodation for an oil company, and renamed Princewall House.

HUTCHEON STREET

From Causewayend to "Killing Hoose" Corner (George Street), and from there past the old station ticket office to Westburn Road

NAMED AFTER Hugh Hutcheon, an influential advocate.

To most Aberdonians, the street is associated with "the Broadford Lum" and "the Killing Hoose", where "the killers" dined out on trestles, under the meat-hooks.

This was a busy street with the heavy carts laden with cowhorn from the harbour, heading for the Combworks, where there were a selection of some three hundred items on display. Export orders were despatched to the zulus, and head-hunters all over the world may still prize combs, handmade, in Aberdeen.

 Huntly Street, and St. Mary's Roman Catholic Cathedral, where there were "splendid altars in marble and Caen Stone".

JOHN STREET

From Loch Street to Woolmanhill

WHERE THE Church of Scotland and the Congregational chapel once had a devout following.

The North of Scotland Bank was erected on the George Street Corner in 1873, to cater for "the steadily increasing business of the cattle trade."

Carters frequented John Street, because near the Woolmanhill, Wordies had a depot. Every morning, fleets of horse lorries left Wordies for the railway station by way of the Denburn Road.

"On John Street corner over a century ago, Mrs Tait lifted a smith's anvil by the hair of her head"; when the crowd was large enough to pass round the cap, "She had a display of knife and fork swallowing at her sideshow." When she gave up, the picture house provided entertainment for folk from the Gallowgate and round about.

Yellow pine moulds were precast here, corner pieces and centre pieces for every ceiling in the city.

🐟 Justice Lane, looking towards the Salvation Army Citadel tower.

JUSTICE MILLS
From Union Glen to Justice Mill Lane

THE "POL' MUIR" wasn't far away from Justice Mill; where the twenty-three-year-old adventurer from "Red Beard's Cave", Durris, was seen dressed as a woman, during December, 1787. This was the last time that Peter Young tried to release prisoners from the Aberdeen Tolbooth, and shortly afterwards he paid the penalty for his crimes on the "Embro'" Scaffold.

JUSTICE STREET
From Castle Street to Park Street

CHAPEL COURT, near the Justice Port, was more renowned as Skipper Scott's Close. He was a sea captain who was the last person in the burgh to have the honour of entertaining a Royal Stuart on December 23rd, 1715. Many Aberdonians who visit that memorial pyramid outside "the Kirk of the Holy Rude" at Stirling, or see Canova's memorial to the family at St. Peter's Rome admit to a strange feeling of the Pretenders' "blood" calling them.

The "poor sisters of Nazareth" arrived at Chapel Court on 14th February 1862, where their service to city children is commemorated along with the titular bishops of Eretria and Morocco.

William Thom, author of "The Mitherless Bairn", and similar touching poems, was born in Sinclair's Close, Justice Street. Poet, John Bruce, who wrote "The Bruce", had his roots here too. Justice Lane ran from East North Street to Justice Street, where the market stance is today. "The fruit cart belonging to Billy Bruce stands in the foreground of the picture", writes Jock Mearns. "The house on the right-hand side of the lane was where Lebbie Annan bided . . . surely washing day with the smoking lum. Mr Robertson's bantam chased away strangers. Madam Rutherford, the Fortune Teller who stayed in the house on the far left, was visited by 'The Theatre People' on gigs dressed to high heavens".

🐟 Lower Justice Mill.
The Holburn provided motivation for the water wheels of both Upper and Lower Justice Mills. Old Mill Road led to the Mill-toun which was surrounded by croftlands. Maids no longer rinse their claes in the cauld mill lade, which since 1931 has run underground.

KING STREET

From Castle Street to Bridge of Don

LONG ENOUGH for the fire brigade horses to get up enough speed, for the children that followed to see sparks flying from their hooves.

The fire station itself looks like a Renaissance palace, and with the North Kirk of 1831 is still worthy of its royal name. (The king in Question was George III).

The hotel proprietor who made the name of the Royal Atheneum was chosen by Jimmy Hay. He was John Mitchell, who, with his wife ran the County Hotel in King Street. The country buses stopped here to collect passengers, who wisely fortified themselves before braving the "caul' gabs o' May" on the Newburgh road. Jean Baxter wrote that on "gaun' hame fae the toon" that the wind outside was as cutting as a knife, but inside, "the burlin' bus is cosy; in beddit stra' the fermer's wife aneth her bonnet's dosy."

King Street was famous for its family businesses. Before the bank building was erected, there was a matching block to the one opposite which was originally John E. Esslemont's "family grocers and Italian warehouse". They were pioneers in the tea trade, and one of the first in the country to receive Ceylon tea. To attract the public, apprentices dressed in pigtails and packed the tea in a well dressed window display. "Tired? We'll refresh you 'good as gold'," was their slogan.

George Washington Wilson's  photograph of the Balaclava cannon, street porters and a hurdy gurdy man, whose monkey strode round on its hindlegs, to the sound of a martial air, showing to advantage the Highland costume in which he was arrayed.

John Street Corner.

On Tuesday 11th April, 1911, the largest consignment of sweets ever to come so far north, meant that this was the opportunity to advertise. Esslemonts hired a piper for the occasion, and Mr John Minty led the procession, with an impressive show of the workforce of the shore posters. Twenty-two horse lorries were used.

The street was always bustling. There were barracks where the bus station is now and frequently there was an industrial haze from brass foundries and train smoke. The number of coaches and carriers' carts that crowded the bridge of Don were reduced when the Buchan and Formartine railway opened.

The Newburgh horsebus at the County Hotel, King Street.

THE INVERSNECKY FIREMAN
from the Singing of Harry Gordon

Ower in Inversnecky, man, we're afa up to
   date,
We've a picture hoose and public hoose,
   that's open very late,
An' noo we've got a fire brigade, an engine
   an' a hose,
An' we practice every Wednesday in oor
   new firemen's clothes.

CO-OPERATIVE MILK MAKES MITES MIGHTY

So if ye have an accident and set your hoose
   on fire
Wi' a lighted match or else a smokey flue,
Ye canna dae much better than send us a' a
   letter
An' we'll come roon if we've nothing else
   to do.

"Fire! Fire!" Everybody shouting "Fire!"
A' the people think that we supply them
   ready made
An' it's certain, more or less, that the fire's
   a big success
If ye leave it to the Inversnecky fire brigade.

The fire brigade gave shell shocked horses from the first world war a new lease of life.

KITTYBREWSTER

THE NAME of one of Aberdeen's lost villages, today means a suburb to some, a cattle mart to others; but to "Kitty" folk themselves it evokes memories of the passenger station and freight terminus. Trainloads of farmers steamed in for the bull and gimmer sales. Weatherbeaten shepherds wearing plaidies were sometimes seen in the company.

Gimmer Sale, 6th September 1926, with Berty Anderson in the rostrum. Seventeen thousand were sold that day.

"It wid tak' a pooir o' neeps tae feed them up fer the bootcher, min."

KITTY BREWSTER by William Cadenhead

She sellt a dram—I kent her fine—
Oot on the road tae Hilton,
Afore the door there stood a sign,
Ahint a lairack beltin'.
The sign tae mak' it bricht an' gay
Taxed Tinte's best resources,
An ale-stoup an' a wisp o' hay—
"Farin' for men and horses".
Her dram wis guid, but O, her ale,
'Twas it that did her credit,
Aboon a' brewsts it bore the bell,
An' 'twas hersel' that made it;
Jist twa-three waughts o't wi' a frien',
Oot ower a bargain makin',
Wad cheer yer hert an' licht your een,
An' set yer lugs a' crackin'.
Her yaird had midden-cocks an' game,
An' mony a cacklin' rooster;
She wis a canty, kindly dame,
They ca'd her Kitty Brewster.

At brewin' time her mashin' tubs
Had sic a mauty flavour,
It gar'd the gabs o' drouthy swabs
Rin ower wi' langin' slaver;
An', fan the browst wis sweet an' new
It sae slid ower the wizzen,
Ye thocht ye war in bliss—yer pow
Had sic a pleasant bizzin'.
An' syne she whang'd the kebbuck doon,
An' cakes het frae the griddle,
While some blythe chap struck up a tune
Upon the cheery fiddle;
An' Kate hersel' wis nivver sweer,
If ony ane induced her,
Tae fit it deftly on the fleer—
Kind, canty Kitty Brewster.

Her kitchen had a fireplace lairge,
A deep recess an' cozey,
Wad haud a dizzen in its mairge,
A' canty and jocosey.
This wis the place in winter keen
For mony a crack political,
Fin dykers had their day's darg deen,
An' state affairs were critical;

An' sae they managed the debate—
They couldna been correcker
Had they been Meenisters o' State,
Or Chancellors o' Exchequer;
An' aye to fill anither jug
Her Parliament induced her,
By whisperin' somethin' in her lug
That pleased kind Kitty Brewster.

Alas, the cheenge! hooses, like men,
Have jist their life to live it;
Kind Kitty's canty but-an'-ben
Is levelled wi' the divot.
Nae mair o' mashin' maut the smell
Sets drouthy mou's a-slaverin'
On yon road side; ye couldna tell
Whaur stood the cozey tavern.
There's naethin' noo bit cattle roups,
An' smells o' meltit tallow,
Whaur ance war filled the reamin' stoups
Tae mony a herty fallow.
I fear that they their wits wad tine,
Wi' train an' locomotive,
The chaps wha ance at Kitty's shrine,
Pour'd their libations votive.
Kate's brewin' craft an' spotless fame—
For nane hae e'er traduced her—
We own fan Lily Bank we name
Conjoined wi' Kitty Brewster.

("For the information of strangers, who, wondering at the peculiar name of the first station on the Great North of Scotland Railway, often ask as to its origin." Folk were sent on a "wild goose chase" by this poem, because no such kindly brewster-wifie existed. Gaelic language Academics have put the record straight concerning the derivation of this place-name.)

"Aw'm a porter at the station,
an' aw like mi occupation;
Chaffin a' the lassies is a job
that suits me clean—
If it's nae the bell aw'm ringin'
ye'll be sure tae hear me singin':
'Cheenge fir Kittybrewster,
Cove or Aiberdeen'."

LANGSTANE PLACE
From Crown Street to Bon-Accord Terrace

ORIGINALLY REFERRED to as the head of Dee Street, where the Langstane is actually situated.

The landmark of the Langstane Kirk, with its beadle's house and cathedral glass was opened in 1869.

Outsiders used to be met at The Lang Stane; a stone's throw from the Toun.

LINKS STREET
From St. Clement Street to The Links

LOOKED OUT OVER the old racecourse. This may have been the place where "Annie" in the Charlie Mackie ballad was "scarcely a week in Aberdeen, when just below her lodgings, when Annie wid tak' the doctor's advice, and tak' a session tae the bathing." The heavy industry that has now taken over Futty's Myre district would not be considered an ideal place for a cure.

"Oh dear me, fit will I dae if I dee an aul' maid in a garret." Gilcomston's first tenement block in Leadside Road, where "longtails" went in search of household pets.

LITTLE BELMONT STREET

From Back Wynd to Belmont Street

WHERE PURCHASES were deposited for out of town delivery for the carrier. There was a smell of singed hoof and tar at the smiddy, where the apprentices' first lesson was to "cha' bogie roll". Boys who attended the town's new schools here thought that Aberdeen was the capital of Scotland.

Ma Cameron's Inn is one of the few bars to survive from the coaching age. Even though its peat fires are a thing of the past in its "snug," until recently the stables in the old cobbled courtyard survived with the faded names of horses on timber posts.

A man worked late in the corner shop, putting marbles into the top of lemonade bottles.

"There wis a mannie an' a wifie,
and they were corkin' bottlies;
says the mannie tae the wifie:'
keekle cackle cocklies".

Ma Cameron's farin' for men an' horses. Timmer Market wares are sold at the door, whilst business is transacted with the carrier inside.

LITTLEJOHN STREET

From Gallowgate to West North Street

WAS PART of the Gallowgate hubbub. John Blaikie's metalworks here made workmanlike bridges. They were respected as bell and brass founders, but worked in copper as well.

THE OLD CO-OP, LOCH STREET

THE ARCADE could also be entered from The Gallowgate. "It was very handy, as you could get everything under the one roof. In those days, a voucher was issued for purchases which could include bakery sundries, groceries, butcher meat, shoes, clothes, bedding, furniture, fancy goods, china, toys and games. When I first kept the family budget, three pounds ten shillings would stock my cupboards for the week."

Mystic and dim; the Co-opie Arcade.

LOCH STREET

From Crooked Lane and Harriet Street to Spring Garden

BIG LOCH STREET, where as the rhyme recalls, "there is a happy land, not so far away", kept clean-scrubbed by smiling ladies, who in exchange for a ticket gave those in need "soup in a bowlie, a slice o' breid and meatbane stew; with a cup o' tea, what mair wid ye expect fir free".

In a shop opposite, "Candy Bell" sold owls' eye eggs, cupid whispers and conversation lozenges. Pink peardrops gleamed like jewels in glass jars, and near a tray of treacle dabs, a white parrot kept watch, biting the children who dared touch it.

The street became a household name, not only for the factory of "Soapy" Ogston, but for the co-op Arcade. "The Coopie" had eight motor delivery vans before the first world war, but children were even quicker at running the odd message to either "the butter side" or "the sugar side", and any Aberdonian worth his salt remembers his mother's "Coopie number".

The Old Co-op, Loch Street, 1883.

LITTLE LOCH STREET. Harness makers and saddlers sat in lofts, repairing or relining traces and collars for small firms to have them ready for the following morning. When work at the smiddie was slack, a mock set of horseshoes were made, and tips of the trade passed on to apprentices, who were told that "horse's hide is nae use for makin' harness." Showpieces made here had sixteen stitches to the inch, and resin thread was rolled for extra strength.

Saturday mornings, pillow cases were also carried in order to collect "brokeners", the second day bread and biscuits.

An Aberdeen Street Song

I chokit on a tattie, a tattie;
I chokit on a tattie
a' through the tattie soup.

My mither sent for the doctor, the doctor;
my mither sent for the doctor,
a' through the tattie soup.

The doctor said you're dying, you're dying;
the doctor said you're dying,
a' through the tattie soup.

They put me in a coffin, a coffin;
they put me in a coffin,
a' through the tattie soup.

I'm in a deidie holie, a holie;
I'm in a deidie holie,
a' through the tattie soup.

And noo I'm up in Heaven, in Heaven;
and noo I'm up in Heaven,
a' through the tattie soup.

The angels gave me supper, supper;
the angels gave me supper,
a' through the tattie soup.

And what I got for supper, for supper;
and what I got for supper,
wis a plate o' tattie soup.

Loch Street Soup Kitchen.

The Hem makers of Little Loch Street,
William Wilson, his son, messrs
Youngson and MacRae at Littlejohn's
workshop on Harriet Street corner with
a set of hems and nickel peakit collars.
The shop in Back Wynd sold silver top
whips to the livery stables in Large
Loch Street, where there were also
straw dealers. Cartloads of fodder for
Aberdeen's horses passed this way.
William Bain's ostlers from Loch
Street fed his horses at Holburn
Junction, where they frequently parked.

LODGE WALK
From Castle Street to Queen Street

DOWN WHICH the grey goose quill-makers of Shoe Lane trundled their
goods to the London Boats. Highland sheep
stealers were watched by the turnkey whilst
they walked round the gaol airing yard. The
nail studded doors of the old Mids o' Mar
prison (otherwise known as the Tolbooth) are
a grim reminder of old fashioned justice.

Public executions in the second half of the
nineteenth century drew a crowd of some
sixteen hundred, so "The Black Calendar of
Aberdeen" records.

Lodge Walk has a special place in the folk-lore heritage of Aberdeen, because the Castle-gate Bobbies who were given tee-names like
"The Tarland Bull", helped to control
obstreperous bairns from one-parent families.

LONG ACRE
From Broad Street to West North Street

A PASSAGEWAY which was one of the
city centre short cuts, leading also to
Henderson's and Jopp's Courts. Wesley
preached here, but his chapel later became a
warehouse.

 Marine Place, Ferryhill.

MARINE TERRACE

From the west side of South Crown Street

ONCE THE HOME of Sea Captains, and amongst the short leet of "Granite City Streets" to have had the first gleaming Bentley limousines standing in readiness outside these "Ferryhill" front doors.

Designed by Archibald Simpson, the terrace was a fine "Look out' over Aberdeen Harbour. Now it is stranded on a yellow bank of daffodils, dreaming of sailing ships; while down the hill at Prospect Terrace, there isn't the "prospect" that there used to be. Young lovers admired the expanse of wild flowers that bloomed, out of reach, over on "The Inches" (islets in the River Dee that survived until the 1880's, when a vast land reclamation plan was carried out; even a scheme to deflect the Dee artifically to the Bay of Nigg was seriously considered).

> "I used tae tak' her walkin' . . .
> oot every single nicht
> doon whaur the river used tae rin;
> an' I told her o sae dearly
> that I loved her so sincerely . . .
> and I'd nivver love anether lass again."
> An excerpt from "Come back Nannie."

 Marine Terrace.   Ferryhill.

MARISCHAL STREET
From Castle Street to Regent Quay

BEFORE 1765, there was no direct public access from Castle Street to the Quay. Consequently the gabled town residence of the Earls Marischal was taken down, and a new street paved with squared granite setts was constructed on arches, which made convenient stables for the new houses. Artists such as the "Pre-Raphaelite", William Dyce, and Andrew Robertson a miniature artist were born here, and at number 46, William Kennedy the advocate wrote "The Annals of Aberdeen" (1818).

Naval Optician's sign, at the foot of Marischal Street.

The solemn perspectives of eighteenth-century Marischal Street.

This was a steep incline, where fire engines had to brake. Bearded sailors came ashore off the whaling boats weaving fur boots, and peered through the dimly lit window of the naval optician. Cattle dealers swiftly arranged for livestock to be sent deck passage to London at the shipping agent's office. The "Aberdeen Line" had twenty vessels with green hulls and yellow funnels at the close of the nineteenth century.

Children wanted to stop at Arthur Courage's shop, for his market candy. Other mouth watering sweets were "soor plooms," cough drops, brandy balls, pear drops, pan drops, all sorts of chocolate, macaroons and Turkish delight.

MARKET STREET

From Union Street to Victoria Bridge

MARKET STREET was laid out 1840-42 and is constructed on arches over the site of an impoverished part of the town known as Putachieside.

Through the steam from the harbour engine's funnel, polo-necked seamen with their black bags over their shoulders headed for the ships. Tracer horses, having hauled loads of steel up the hill, stopped and rested at St. Nicholas Street whilst their chains were removed.

Harness sometimes wouldn't take the gradient, but all went well on July 2nd, 1881, when a procession of the Town Council went in carriages to open the £25,000 Victoria Bridge. The 345 long structure was the pride of John Fyfe, granite merchant of Kemnay. The bridge presents the strange appearance of having two archways through each pier. This is because the masonry was built upon the top of the caissons, and the three small piers joined together above water by two arches.

MARYWELL STREET

From South College Street to Crown Street

A PUBLIC DRAW WELL here, dedicated to St. Mary, was just one of the famous springs of Aberdeen.

It was a century ago that John Ellis, who resided at number eighteen, set up in business as "a coal merchant and commission agent." The industrial estates soon to be laid out on the reclaimed bed of the River Dee, nearby, were a thing of the future.

Egypt moves her temples; Aberdeen, her statues. Now the Market Street pedestrian archways and the Putachieside Portals of the New Market have bitten the dust.

MOUNTHOOLY

From Causewayend to King's Crescent originally, "from Gallowgate to the Canalside"

CROFT LAND, belonging to the church, and therefore deemed Holy; another local croft was "Calsey".

The balcony over the John Knox church door, gives the impression of being an outside pulpit, but only addresses itself to the largest roundabout in Aberdeen. St. Margaret's Convent stands to the north on rising ground, near an ancient holy place, – The Spital.

Those expecting to find the old Mounthooly might exclaim: "is this the hill? is this the Kirk? is this mine own Countrie?".

NELSON STREET

From King Street to West North Street

LAID OUT AT the time of the battle of Trafalgar. The only "charges" that were ever made were by cattle being taken this route to the mart from the Links. Women ran for the safety of shop doors when they heard the pounding of hooves. Mrs Scullion at the corner fish shop sold hot ranns, to the young cinema goers who wished to develop their brains on the way to the Globe cinema.

🐖 NEW MARKET

The refined forcefulness of Archibald Simpson's New market design, (1840-42) "was adapted from the basilicas of Rome".

When it opened on April 29th 1842, choirs and pipebands were in attendance.

You could buy almost anything in this universal store; it was known for its distinct blend of smells. Merchants in the gallery provided a range of trinkets and services. Ears could be pierced, bodies tattooed, watches engraved and fortunes told.

🐖 Mounthooly Convent Chapel, designed by Ninian Comper, son of a local priest.

"Out on an errand for the Sisters of Mercy, she walks warily through the busy throngs of people; her legs carry her slowly decaying temple adorned in deepest black with immaculate whiteness . . . She knew where she was going as she climbed up the precipitous steps of the Mother Convent. She was going home."

An excerpt from "The Old Nun"
by Stanley Robertson.

Much could also be learnt about the city, besides turning the musty pages of leatherbound books that made it seem that the Bodleian Library of Lowe's Bookstall had burst up there in the massive roof.

Children were always to be seen looking into "the penny-in-the-slot" machine at the Union Street lobby, where a fireman gallantly rescued a woman from a burning room. The New Market was itself burnt down despite the efforts of the old handpumps of the firebrigade. When it was reopened, the shareholders voted that the stalls could be let free for a week.

OSBORNE PLACE

From Albert Street to Blenheim Place

FORMERLY North Carden Place, but now keeps green the memory of Victorian High Society. Each household had its servant "living in", who knew all about the Sovereign's entourage (and her politicians), besides keeping all the rooms as clean as the palaces of Sandringham, Balmoral, Windsor and "Osborne", itself, which is on the Isle of Wight.

🐖 Patchy Low's Bookstall at the Newmarket.

Old Mill Road.

OLD MILL ROAD
From Marywell Street to Union Glen

THE MILL referred to is the lower Justice Mill in Union Glen.

PATAGONIAN COURT
From Belmont Street to Denburn Road

MERCHANTS WHO DEALT with their counterparts in Patagonia, brought back their wealth with them by boat, to the back door of their homes in this quarter of the city. The Denburn was tidal at this point.

The old Bleachgreen bath-house at the foot of Patagonian court was the place where one Cove fisherwoman went upon being taken ill with labour pains. She was delivered of twins, whom she stowed carefully in her creel, shouldered it and set off for home. Some dykesides still have a recess for creels to be rested.

The Gaelic congregation, who climbed these stairs to attend chapel, were a close-knit community like the Fisher Folk. Aberdeen respected their culture, and language, but they were left alone.

Patagonian Court Stairs.

PORTLAND STREET

From Crown Street to South College Street

A GREAT PLACE for small business concerns: a granite yard, brickworks, coal merchants, woodmerchant, plasterer, wheelwrights, and stablers, whose cab horses knew their way home when they were hired out.

Wordies had their depot, Cartwright and Smith's shop at Clayhills, besides being at "Roger's Walk" John Street, Schoolhill and Bannermill. The company had 335 horses insured for £175 17s 6d in the 1870's and did business with Aberdour, Banff, MacDuff, Cullen, Cruden Bay, Fraserburgh, Huntly, Inverurie, Lossiemouth, Portsoy, Stonehaven and Turriff. They were linked administratively with Stirling, another large railway haulage concern owned by the same company.

POYNERNOOK ROAD

From Market Street to Palmerston Road

LAID OUT ON LAND once known as the Poyner's Neuk, owned by "the Pynours" (shore Porters).

Tin sheds lined the road, and wooden barrels lined the pavement. Horses delivered the fish and worked from crack of dawn for their masters.

PRINCES STREET

From King Street to Park Street

NEVER CONSIDERED very princely, the coffin carts were seen here rather than royalty.

Town horses used to be shod in ☞ Martin's Lane, south of the Green.

QUEEN'S CROSS

At the junction of Albyn Place, Carden Place, St. Swithin Street, Fountainhall Road, Queen's Road, and Queen's Gardens

WHEN THE statue of Queen Victoria, by C. B. Law (1893) was placed in a regal position, looking towards Balmoral, yet within view of a certain resident's front door, a councillor received a complaint about an "east end personage" being moved to the west end . . . otherwise known as "The Queen".

George Washington Wilson, who was asked to take photographic likenesses of the Royal family, lived at number one Queen's Cross, in a villa shaped like a clover leaf. Russell Mackenzie the architect provided him with a set of weathervanes that had to be greased regularly, and a central heating system. The yellow pine moulds for the cornices and ceiling roses were specially made. Peacocks, thistles and fruit adorned the walls above the brass picture rails. Wallpaper was hand printed, and imported from Italy in tin containers. Woodwork received five coats, and everything was sealed until the painters had finished applying the egg shell enamel.

On his photographic assignments, George Washington Wilson shoed his own horse, ate dried venison and "braxie mutton" (savoury sausages made from sheep found dead in the hills). When he slept out in mountainside bothies his straw bed was sprinkled with cheap and powerful whisky to kill the bugs.

Housekeepers purchased samples of tea from the family grocer and provision merchants Gordon & Smith, and compared brands from their China and Assam tea warehouse with those obtained elsewhere. Their premises at 195-197 Union Street were open from 8 am to 8 pm, Monday to Friday – Saturdays 8 am to 6 pm. Extracts from the price list (189?) are reproduced by kind courtesy of Neil Kerr of Gordon & Smith Catering.

The kitchen at George Washington Wilson's home at Queen's Cross is now a restaurant, "below stairs."

Maids at a West-End doctor's house.

Salt, &c.

			s.	D.
Salt, Finest Kitchen,	.	per stone,	0	4
Do.,	.	per cwt.,	2	0
Table Salt,	.	drums,	0	2½
Do.,	.	jars,	0	5
Do.,	.	bots.,	0	5
Bowie's Nutritive Table Salt,	in packets, 1d., 4d., and		0	8
"Pepsalia" Digestive Table Salt,	„ each, 1s. and		2	0
Eno's Fruit Salt,	.	per bot.,	2	2
Salts Volatile,	.	.	0	7
Bay Salt,	.	per stone,	0	8
Salt of Celery,	.	per bot.,	0	5
Searcy's Salt,	.	„	0	10
Saltpetre, whole,	.	per lb.,	0	4½
Do., ground,	.	„	0	5
Sal-Prunella,	.	„	1	0
Tidman's Salt,	in boxes, 1s. 3d. and		2	0
Bath Salt,	.	per stone,	0	8

Plain and Fancy Brushes.

		EACH.—s.	D.
Hearth, plain, various,	8d., 10d., 1/3, 1/6, and	1	9
Do. fancy, black and gilt,	1/, 1/3, 1/6, 1/9, „	2	6
Shoe, in variety,	6d., 8d., 10d., 1/, 1/3, 1/6, 1/9, „	2	6
Black Lead,	1/1, 1/6, 2/3, „	2	9
Scrubbing,	4d., 6d., 1/, 1/6, 2/3, 2/9, „	3	6
Clothes,	6d., 10d., 1/6, 2/, 2/6, 3/, „	4	6
Plate,	8d., 1/, 1/6, 2/, 2/6, „	3	0
Crumb,	1/, 2/, 2/6, „	3	0

Wooden Wares, &c.

Butter Spoons,	. 3d. to 6d.	American Tubs,	. 1/ to 5/
Cooking Spoons,	. 2d. to 1/	Oak Tubs,	. 3/ to 12/
Flour Pails,	. 2/6 to 5/	Galvanized Pails,	10d. to 1/3
Housemaids' Boxes,	. 2/ to 4/	Do. Baths,	. 1/ to 2/
Washing Boards,	10d. to 1/3	Do. Basins,	10d. to 1/3
Bread Platters,	. 1/6 to 5/	Pulp Basins,	. 2/3
Wooden Spurtles, each,	. 2d.		

Black Lead.

			PER LB. s.	D.
Davies' Peruvian Lustre, in 1 lb., ½ lb., and ¼ lb.,			0	10
Nixey's Block, in squares,	. 1d., 2d., and		0	4
Reckitt's Diamond, in squares, ½d., 1d., and 3d.; and boxes,			0	10
Do., in balls and lump,	. 6d. to		0	8
Davies' British Lustre, packets,	.		0	8
Dome Black Lead, in boxes,	. each,		0	6
Lawson's Black, no black-leading required, dried in 20 minutes, sold in tins, . each, 4½d., 6½d., and			1	0
Enameline, in boxes,	.		0	2½
"Rising Sun" Stove Polish,	. 1d. and		0	2
Zebra Grate Polish,	. 1d., 2d., and		0	5

Oils.

			s. D.	s. D.
Seal Oil, finest,	.	per gallon,	2 6	to 2 8
Colza Oil,	.	„	2 6	to 2 8
Sperm Oil,	.	„	4 6	to 5 0
Paraffin Oil, Young's,	.	„	0 7	to 0 8
Linseed Oil,	.	„	2 6	to 2 8
Castor Oil, in bottles,	.	per bottle,	0 3	to 1 6
Do., for cattle,	.	„	0 10	to 1 0
Cod Liver Oil,	.	„	1/, 1/6, and	2 0
Do., Emulsion,	.	„	3/, „	2 0
Methylated Spirits, for Spirit Lamps,	.	„	.	0 8

Furniture Polish, Blacking, &c.

			s.	D.
Blacking, Day & Martin's,	per bottle, 4d., 8d., and		0	10
Propert's Standard Blacking,	„ 4d., and		0	10
Propert's Royal Navy Dressing, for brown leather, 5d. &			0	10
Kid Reviver,	. bottles, 5d. and		0	10
Brand's Blacking,	. per bottle,		0	10
Brunswick Black,	. 5d. and		0	10
Berlin Black,	. 5d. and		0	10
Lawson's Black, for stoves and grates, is equal to the best Japan for wood and iron, . 4½d., 6½d., and			1	0
Adams' Furniture Polish,	. 5d., 9d., and		1	6
Stevenson's Furniture Polish,	. 5d., 10d., and		1	6
Smith's Furniture Polish,	. 5d., 10d., and		0	10
Needham's Polishing Paste, in pots,	. 1d., 4d., and		0	8
Pickering's Brown Polish, for cleaning and preserving brown leather, in tins, . each, 3d. and			0	6
Household Metal Polish, in tins,	.		0	1
Blanco, a new preparation for whitening tennis and cricket shoes, &c., and with zinc mould, 6d. each; without the mould, 1d. each; or . per doz.,			0	10
Zampo, for cleaning ivory,	. per pkt.,		1	0
Stevenson's Metal Polish Fluid,	. 5d. and		0	10
Globe Metal Polish, in tins,	. 1d. and		0	2½
Goddard's Plate Powder,	. 5d., 10d., and		2	6

Bon-Accord and Aspinall's Enamel.

White.	Red	Terra Cotta.	Blue.
Ivory.	Orange.	Brown.	Walnut.
Coral.	Green.	Black.	Vermilion.
Olive.	Grey.	Canary.	Pink.

The above, and other Enamels, sold in Tins, 6d., 9d., and 1s.

ROSEBANK PLACE (133 HARDGATE)

ROSEBANK HOUSE, an eighteenth century villa, now obscured by "Willowbank", has become a tenement, but in its heyday contributed culturally to the neighbourhood. Owned by the Dyce family, artists and literary men were frequent visitors. It never was as famous as Seaton Cottage, another venue for painters in the public eye, but John Smith, the city architect liked the place, and resided here until his death in 1852.

Royal carriage, Queen's Cross, 1906.

QUEEN STREET
From Broad Street to North Street

NAMED AFTER the Queen of George III; the gracious surroundings have been eradicated. Here was the old playhouse, and the county showed their approval of the place, for Earl Aberdeen's commissioner had a residence here, which later became the office of the "Aberdeen Herald". Latterly, Queen Street's shops — down steps and open late, were a mecca for dealers, who enjoyed a dram at "The Banks of Ythan" and "The Artillery Arms".

Aberdeen Herald's office, Queen Street. ☞

RICHMOND STREET
From Leadside Road to Rosemount Place

A TENEMENT STREET that has survived nearly intact from the 1870's. Built of coursed rubble, it predates the Golden Age of tenement building, 1880-1910.

ROSEMOUNT PLACE
From Skene Square to Beechgrove Terrace

FORMERLY A COUNTRY ROAD (from Farmers' Hall Lane to Mile End being garden ground, with spacious villas like "Belvidere" and "Wallfield", standing in their own policies).

A tracer horse was required at Stevenson Street to haul the open deck horse tram up the brae to Wallfield. William Bain's horse buses had served the district until 1872; later a single track was laid from the North Kirk (King Street), to Queen's Cross. With this, came the "Rosemount Improvements". Crescents, and an avenue of imperious tenements.

ROSEMOUNT SQUARE
Bounded by South Mount Street, Leadside Road, Richmond Street and Kintore Place

ORIGINALLY THIS was the Aladdin's Cave of Cocky Hunter's store, but this perished in a fire, and was replaced by the model flats, which appropriately have granite sculptures of the elements placed over arched entrances.

ROSE STREET

From "Union Place to the Bridewell" now from Union Street to Skene Street

UNION PLACE was the Harley Street of Aberdeen, whose doctors ordered carriages from John Clark whose workshop was just round the corner here. He was the proud originator of the "Beatrice phaeton", and as his Royal Appointment indicated, "The Victoria" described as a "sociable phaeton", and "The Empress", were well received. He supplied "Glasgow polocarts", "stanhope gigs on five springs", as well as "village gigs", "O gee pony traps" and "the reversible waggonette".

There was also a pleasure garden as well as the Bridewell prison in Rose Street.

"Home home sweet lodgings sweet spirits and sweet ale that ever be so humble – there's nae place like the gaol. When your red eyed wife is weeping and your offsprings a' join in. Then its time to tie yer whiskers an' whistle through yer chin.

I got a letter from sweet Catherine that made my cheeks grow pale – she said that she would marry me when she comes out of gaol – she said when we are man and wife I'd hae nae cause tae groan – for if I supply a cradle – she has umpteen babes of her own".

Rose Street in 1883, showing the Gateway to the Bridewell prison. The houses in the foreground have survived, and recently were refurbished.

ROSEMOUNT VIADUCT
From Schoolhill to South Mount Street

JUSTLY FAMED for its public buildings. Originally there was just the Public Library and St. Marks. Now the Theatre makes up the trio known as "Education, Salvation and Damnation".

The Skene Street and Baker Street portion of the quarter of a mile crescent was completed first, and is built on arches. The scale of the throughfare means that Upper Denburn Bridge is twenty-five feet above street level. The sixteen foot statue of William Wallace is attached to a pedestal of "Corennie Steens," and iron rods are his arteries. A spare hand is kept in store for beckoning purposes; Piranesi would have approved of the Viaduct.

The public library building, marooned like a granite liner. Librarians looked out of the portholes into the garret windows of Little Skene Street.

The quart jugs jingle as he walks the street
puir milk laddie wi' blistered feet;
though Wallace looks doon in muckle prime
it's a lang day laddie tae lousing time.

He gangs tae hooses, shops and stairs
he passes ithers selling wares;
he whistles, diddles, laughs at rhyme –
it's a lang day laddie tae lousing time.

(Thoughts by Stanley Robertson about the most meaningful photo in the book to him.)

"The Dawn of Light and Liberty."
John D. Stephen's art photo of a milk cairt loon dwarfed by the Wallace Statue. Country buses started from here early in the morning too.

127

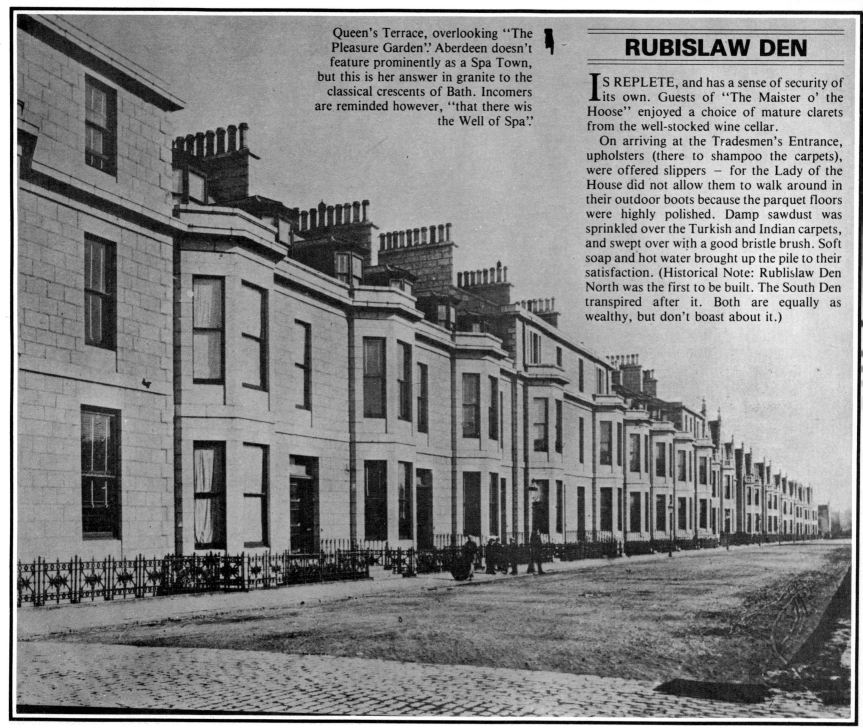

Queen's Terrace, overlooking "The Pleasure Garden". Aberdeen doesn't feature prominently as a Spa Town, but this is her answer in granite to the classical crescents of Bath. Incomers are reminded however, "that there wis the Well of Spa".

RUBISLAW DEN

IS REPLETE, and has a sense of security of its own. Guests of "The Maister o' the Hoose" enjoyed a choice of mature clarets from the well-stocked wine cellar.

On arriving at the Tradesmen's Entrance, upholsters (there to shampoo the carpets), were offered slippers – for the Lady of the House did not allow them to walk around in their outdoor boots because the parquet floors were highly polished. Damp sawdust was sprinkled over the Turkish and Indian carpets, and swept over with a good bristle brush. Soft soap and hot water brought up the pile to their satisfaction. (Historical Note: Rubislaw Den North was the first to be built. The South Den transpired after it. Both are equally as wealthy, but don't boast about it.)

Some Aberdeen sayings. (Nannies' advice to their young charges).

"Never speak about your own concerns. When things go wrong with you, folk are not just terribly sorry; and if you are prospering, folk are not so glad as you would think."

"A man's a man till he owes you money, then you meet a stranger."

"If people are speaking about you, they are not speaking about anybody else."

"When there's good times, think about the hard times."

"He had nae soles to his boots, and a lame horse, but he could aye mak' a living."

Poverty to wealth in three generations. Wealth to poverty in three generations.

A friend in need, is a friend that you are better without.

Jist 'cause there's snaw on the roof; it disna mean the fire's oot.

Rubislaw Terrace, where retired colonels chose to live. The novelist Baron Corvo lodged in rooms down Union Street nearby, and referred to well disciplined rows of houses such as these as being mere "granite rabbit hutches."

ST. ANDREW STREET

From Loch Street to Woolmanhill

FORMERLY SHUTTLE STREET, this district was the weaver's quarter. The former Demonstration School, now Robert Gordon's Institute changed the character and scale of the place. The Burking house that stood here, was destroyed by angry townsfolk; but the fear of being taken away for dissection by the anatomists persisted well into this century.

 Parade of the Voluntary Red Cross Ambulance drivers, 1918, looking towards Crooked Lane.

ST. CLEMENT STREET

From Miller Street at Garvock Wynd, to York Place

BUILT IN THE promising days of wooden ships and iron men. The marine architecture of the Foot Dee warehouses, and the constrasting straight-laced kirk built in 1826, are reminders of a grandiose scheme for the district which included a square and other amenities looking out over the busy harbour fairway so that merchants wives could see their ships come sailing in. The idea died with them, but a walk around the churchyard is a proof of Aberdeen's determined achievement in shipbuilding history.

In 1853 the clipper *Cairngorm* refused to be launched; whereupon squads of shipwrights jumped up and down on the deck to no avail. They enlisted the aid of armed forces from Castlehill Barracks, who hauled her down the slipway obligingly.

ST. NICHOLAS STREET

From Union Street to George Street

HERE STOOD "The Queen", and it was the place to catch the subby tram. The original Fowler's London Rubber shop opened in St. Nicholas Street, and demonstrations with a hose to show the worthiness of the products were a novelty.

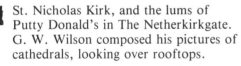 St. Nicholas Kirk, and the lums of
Putty Donald's in The Netherkirkgate.
G. W. Wilson composed his pictures of
cathedrals, looking over rooftops.

St. Nicholas Street "Subby" Tram
Terminus, and "Clippies".

 The old Grammar School, Schoolhill.

"Sillerton Laddies" at Schoolhill.

SCHOOLHILL
From Upperkirkgate to Woolmanhill

WHERE CHILDREN thought that the art gallery statues were taken out for a wee wee. Plaster cast classical athletes were at one time, a feature of the gallery forecourt.

The chestnut vender, who took up his stance on Harriet Street corners had a warm fire going, but one customer would have just warmed his hands and not parted with a single bawbie – this was Robert Gordon who built the famous "old hoosie" (later known as Fort Cumberland). It was said of him that he once bored a hole in the floor of his room, so that he could read by the light of the cobbler who lived below. On another occasion he was spoken about after he had squeezed a mouse dry that had fallen into a jug of milk.

The old Grammar School bell summoned children to school here (1757-1883) – one of the famous pupils was Lord Byron.

Burnett Carr, the gravedigger, stayed here.

Schoolhill, and Jamesone's Hoose. 👉

SHOE LANE
From West North Street to Queen Street

THE NAME commemorates the work of the Shoemaker craft.

SKENE SQUARE
From Gilcomston Steps to Caroline Place

AN OLD turnpike road, once flanked by pantiled cottages, where one sink on the stairs served several households. John "Spanish" Phillip's birth place was demolished, and replaced with morbid tenements.

Wellhead of "The Skene Raw Wallie" 👉 – rebuilt opposite Rubislaw Terrace Gardens. The ice-cold water of the spring well of St. John of Jerusalem mingled well with strong whisky "tae mak' mony a guid cuppie o' Birse Tea" for Upper Denburn Folk.

SOUTH CONSTITUTION STREET

"THERE WIS cork makin', electric weldin'; and those that told yer name – Davy Stewart had a painting on his door, that wis his wye o' telling fowk, aboot lead, zinc, an' flame".

SPRINGBANK

A WATERSHED between Crown Street and Hardgate. On rising ground stands Willowbank.

"A boorachie o' loons" in Schoolhill.

SUGARHOUSE LANE
From Regent Quay to Virginia Street

BUILT IN THE mid eighteenth century when the new industry of sugar refining was introduced into Scotland – the four "shipping towns" of Glasgow, Greenock, Dundee and Aberdeen opened up considerable trade with the Southern States of America and the West Indies. It is from this industrial movement, that the names of Virginia Street and Sugarhouse Lane arose.

Guiseppe Bordone, celebrated seller of hot chestnuts and ice cream. "Yorkie" also won the hearts of passers-by with a performance of chanting and snatches on his mouth organ; a few bright pennies always covered the bottom of a new year's biscuit tin that was tied round his neck with a cord.

"See him coming doon the street,
gymnastics on his feet,
the only man in Aiberdeen,
the only man to mak' ice cream."

An Aberdeen Street Song
"A penny's o' chips tae grease m' lips;
one, two, three . . ."

134

THEATRE LANE

From Regent Quay to Virginia Street

"BY THE lamplight, lonely, gleaming –
by the corner of the lane,
stands a lovely, lonely maiden –
'come, who will buy my pretty flowers?'."

The match and flower girls stood by the back door of the theatre, and sold their wares to performers. Then moved stance to the front door of "The Old Bandbox" in Marischal Street. They saw Paganini arrive at the changing rooms to give a concert. The deep impression "his wax-coloured face, long streaming hair, and the mysterious expression his eyes made," followed his audience home.

Theatre Lane, behind Marischal Street. Stable facilities survive, under houses built by William "Sink-'em" Smith.

UNION GLEN

**From Springbank Terrace
to Cuparstone Row**

IF IT WERE STILL the day of the horse in the city, this place would be a massive. stable. Instead it is turned over to motor cars and light industry.

A few cottages survive behind the Holburn Street frontages, but they postdate the Clachan of the wooden cup-makers.

UNION GROVE

From Holburn Street to Forest Avenue

FAMOUS FOR ITS front parlours replete with pianoforte. The light and shadow of the place is perhaps a quality which makes this a memorable street. A corner of Aberdeen that will always be surreal. It was at number 42, that James McBey pulled his first copper-

plate etching (a simple study of Point Law loons) on the laundry mangle. When he was working at the George Street branch of the North of Scotland Bank (see John Street photograph).

Union Grove mansion and its landscaped grounds were planned to be yet another city park. Instead they were obliterated.

The bustle of Union Street. ☞
The water-cairts, the taxi cabs,
an' twa-decked tramway cars,
the spacious shops an' offices,
the kirks an' drinkin' bars.

UNION STREET

"Frae Castlegate to Ba'bie Law"

THE SOUND OF HARNESS, and the voices of ostlers could be heard, as William Bain who was strapper to the Defiance coach, hurriedly prepared the carriages for their departure. This traffic, and the bustle of people thronging the street on summer evenings further delayed the horse trams on their single track, when the eighty strong, fourth Aberdeen Artillery, Volunteer Citizen company, wearing dark green uniform, marched from gun practice at the Beach Battery. They were dismissed in the gas-lit stable yard behind the massive water house.

When they took customers to an "At Home" dance, cabbies waited outside in groups, smoking their short clay "cheek-warmers", "yarnin' o' men an' horses intae the sma' oors".

Guests were warmed by "soup on departure," and were well inclined to hand over a tip for the price of a bottle of stout, or a chew of tobacco. News was passed around about obstreporous clients who had only the dawn chorus to keep them company when thrown into the horse trough.

🐟 Union Place (now Union Street).

When the snow set in, private sleighs with bells were brought out. Bakers' vans were mounted on runners, and goods traffic required the aid of tracer horses. The tramcar company used rough wooden horsedrawn sledges that carried twenty people; at stopping places, those in the back were in danger of being shot off.

Sometimes there were temporary exhibitions in empty shops, such as the short lived display of taxidermy by the naturalist Thomas Edward, with the centrepiece of "The Death of Cock Robin", set on a mossy hillock surmounted by the killer equipped with a bow held in one claw, and an arrowcase slung across his wing; Robin Readbreast lay on his back, with his feet in the air. Stuffed mice and pheasants were taken away to be sold by six carrier carts, before they had a chance to become fashionable under gleaming glass domes, and joined the stuffed pets that graced the homes of old ladies.

Queen Victoria affectionately referred to "My neighbours of Aberdeen", and remembered one tradesman in particular; the hatter Samuel Martin, who advertised in doggrel verses. When he stood at his open window wearing a red Garibaldi shirt, as Her Majesty's coach passed by, she heard his name mentioned and said approvingly of this patriotic gentleman with the waxed moustaches, "that is the little hatter".

An English excursionist writing "The Land we live in", remarked about the spacious rooms in his hotel near Union Bridge; having on arrival noticed the clean brass doorplate and flowing muslin curtains at first floor windows. At table there was delicious bread, "white as driven snow, and as light, with fresh butter worked into swans, Scottish lions and cupids". Coachguards were at the hotel on the appointed hour, active and courteous in red coats and hats. Outside the colonnaded Royal Hotel and Posting House, portmanteaus and guncases blazing with crest or coronet, indicated a departure to The Highlands.

Visitors sometimes thought that the fisher-women's mutches were "tall Flemish caps" and were interested to see their "foreign looking ear-rings".

Jewellers' shops shone in the sunlight; "a perfect blaze of wealth and ornamental beauty in the rings, chains, crosses, brooches and seals cut from the mineral productions of Aberdeenshire". In the morning, shopkeepers arrived in top hat and coat, and often stood at the door to welcome customers with a bow, or by shaking hands. A chuckle was in their case the height of exuberance. Their vocabulary was weighed out and dealt more in negatives than affirmatives. If phenomenally prosperous they described the position as "nae that ill ava", as they escorted customers personally to their cab.

The Regency Screen by City Architect John Smith, 1830. From here radiated milestones to outlying villages.

Union Street celebrates the Union of Great Britain and Ireland which occurred in 1800, the same year as the Act for bridging the Denburn was passed. This is history, not matrimonials, however. *Walkin' the Mat* created a lasting bond between those who "clicked" down the lover's lane of Union Street. As long as you had money for a cafe and a bus fare that was the only outlay you had to think about as the tram turned the corner of Holburn Junction or clanked to a halt at "The Queen", on the corner of St. Nicholas Street. Maybe it was an illusive wisp of train smoke reaching for the stars beyond the "Monkey House" or the bright chalk of pavement pictures, that made their hearts strangely warm. Granny could not spoil the feeling of anticipation of young "Northern lights" even if she tried throwing a candlestick if they arrived back home after ten, for often, wedding rings that were sold by weight were already chosen. Girls in service were similarly restricted by time on their evening out.

"The Mat" was the southern pavement between the Athenaeum and Market Street; "The Carpet" was the section from Market Street to Bridge Street. Older onlookers were there to bide even if nobody was waiting for them at the "Monkey House", "Student's Corner", "The Catwalk" or "The Queen."

"For lovely girls often meet new loves
you can go to the market
you can go to the fair;
you can go to the church
on Sunday and meet your love there"

An excerpt from a ballad, "Young Molly."

Today, C&A's Corner impresses less than the marble stairs in Incorporated Trades Hall or Palace Hotel facing it. If important guests wanted quiet, peat was laid to muffle the cabs.

"it's the win', the win' blaws high,
the rain comes dashin' frae the sky.
for puir Maggie she must die
for her lover in the Golden Sky —
she is handsome, she is pretty,
she is the girl of the Silver City —
she has lovers one two three —
come and tell me who they be."

"HOW OUR GIRLS KISS"

The Rubislaw girl bows her stately head
And fixes her stylish lips
In a firm, hard way, and lets 'em go,
And sips, and sips and sips.

The Rosemount girl takes off her specs
So cool, so cool, so glum,
She sticks out her lips like an open book,
And keeps on chewing gum.

The Torry girl never says a word
She's so gentle, timid and tame
But she grabs a young man by the back of the
    neck
And gets there just the same.

The Woodside girl has a way of her own
In a clinging, soulful way
She takes a kiss that is just as big
As a wagon-load of hay.

The Ferryhill girl gets a grip on herself
And carefully takes off her hat
Then grabs the man in a frenzied way
Like a terrier shaking a rat.

An Aberdeen girl gives a wonderful kiss
In Fittie or Kittybrewster
But, being married, I can't tell if they kiss
As often as they use 'ter.

> — a few words from Harry Gordon
> at the Beach Pavilion, 1924.

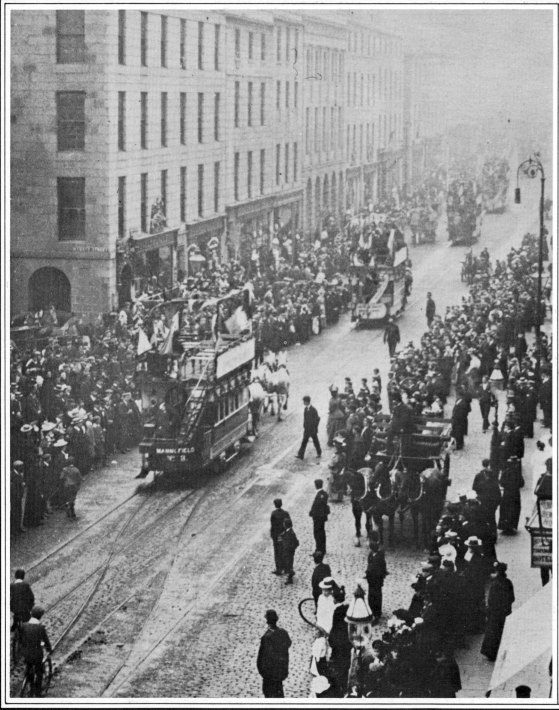

Procession of horsedrawn trams, 1898.

I'm the auldest man that's ever lived in
 Aiberdeen,
An' lots an' lots o' famous things an' people I
 hae seen.
I can min' fin Wallace in oor ceety spent an
 'oor,
I went an' hid a drink wi' him inside "The
 Wallace Toor".

Chorus:
Fittie fowk, Kitty fowk, Kwintra fowk an'
 Ceety fowk,
Fowk fae Constitution Street, an' fowk fae
 Rubislaw Den,
Wallfield, Nellfield, Mannofield, an'
 Cattofield,
List' tae local stories that professors dinna
 ken.

I can min' fin Shakespeare cam' here wi' a
 traivellin' show;
They chairged ye for admission, so, of course,
 I didna go.
I min' Henry VIII arrivin' in his royal gig,
And caravans wi' Henry's wives stretched a'
 the wye t' Nigg. — *Chorus.*

I can min' on Hazleheid afore there wis a tram;
I can min' fin Mr Walker first said Walker's
 Dam;
I can min' fin folk wis hangt beside the
 Market Cross;
I can min' fin there wis peacocks doon in
 Peacock's Closs. — *Chorus.*

I can min' afore the perfume fact'ry cam' t'
 Cove;
I can min' the time there wis nae bairns in
 Union Grove.
Lots o' ither things I'd min' if I hid time t'
 think —
Bit I canna min' fin onybody offered me a
 drink. — *Chorus.*

An excerpt from "The Auldest Aiberdonian"
(From the singing of Harry Gordon; words
and music by Forbes Hazlewood).

UNION TERRACE
From Union Terrace to Rosemount Viaduct

FARMERS STOOD in amazement to see Clydesdale tracer horses curvetting with heavy loads, nervous of the clanking trams and the whistle of steam engines.

The pavements rang with the sound of tacketted parish boots, but in 1932, The Caledonian Hotel confidently promised guests, "freedom from the irritation of extreme traffic noises; seclusion without being cloistered".

Old men sat and fed the pigeons.

🐟 Union Terrace Gardens – known as "The Trainie Park".

URQUHART ROAD
From King Street to Links Road

A TENEMENT STREET, famous for its Hogmanay festivites. In the summer, East End folk walked to the beach past "sma' shoppies", that hung childrens' buckets and spades outside their doors. On the way, the Gordon Highlanders might be seen on parade at The Links.

Young pupils at King Street public school proudly made needlework samplers, demonstrated darns, and could "turn a heel" well. All high quality workmanship – sad to relate, there was high infant mortality rate, and nearby "Cuningarhill" was built as a fever hospital. It is an ancient saying that if toonsfolk had a malady, they must be "put to the Links". During the plague years, many mass graves were dug there.

On a more cheerful note, the famous Dr. Walford Bodie was born here. Hypnotist, cartooner, conjureror and ventriloquist, he claimed that the "MD" stood for "Merry Devil".

VICTORIA STREET
From Albyn Place to Skene Street

BUILT IN the days of the young Queen. Archibald Simpson's Terrace is simplicity in granite design. James Scott Skinner resided here, and played his stroch violin to the delight of those who admired his fiery brilliance. The granite trade considered that many a good tune is played on an old fiddle, so extra care was taken with "the grain of the granite" on "The Strathspey King's memorial".

VIRGINIA STREET
From Weigh-house Square to Commerce Street

SPRING TIDES have reached this point, but the whole place was a miracle of engineering design, and the Marischal Street flyover otherwise known as Bannerman's Bridge is still safe, even though it was erected as early as 1766.

The slopes below Castlegate were congested with buildings until 1978. St. Clement's Manse with its postern gate, approached up a flight of stairs was a pleasant feature surrounded by more gaunt commercial buildings. Bonded stores, built to last for ever have made way for a ring road. The original members of the Melville United Free Church first worshipped in a converted warehouse on the corner of Virginia Street and Weigh-house Square. It has been said that some of the Aberdeen Kirks look like schools, but this was the only one that looked like a warehouse.

🐟 Once past the Brig o' Dee and the Mill o' Leggart, Robert Burns, on ascending the Causey Mounth Highway, turning in his saddle and surveying Aberdeen said, it was "a lazy toun".

143

👉 The old weigh-house, where street porters plied for work. Wordie's chiels and fellow cairters were on call nearby.

WAPPING STREET

**From Trinity Street to Lower Denburn
(Now removed)**

PROBABLY NAMED after old fashioned fishermens' garb, rather than its Thameside equivalent.

Wapping Street contained the first Gas Office. Nearby were wood-merchants' yards where the first circular saw driven by horse was introduced to Aberdeen. A calendar mill where "a man or woman did a spell of duty as a turnspit dog," makes this street an ideal subject for a working display in an open air museum.

WEIGH-HOUSE SQUARE

THE ORIGINAL seventeenth century "Pack" house was demolished to make way for the Harbour Board Offices which are built partially over the old square.

A timber platform was built with material salvaged from a wreck of an Amsterdam vessel which ran ashore on the Belhelvie sands. The upper floor was used as a sail loft. Unclaimed merchandise such as bales of wool, chests of tea, indigo, crockery and bars of steel were stored there: The walls were three feet thick. This was also a hay store, so men tethered their horses before going inside. Weigh-house and Pack house-dues had to be paid.

WOMBELL'S MENAGERIE

Wombwell's Menagerie was always welcomed to the city, and during the few days of its stay was greatly patronised. There were about 30 caravans, in which the wild beasts were confined and housed, and these were placed in the form of a square, where the exhibition took place. Sometimes this was in the Woolmanhill, near the Royal Infirmary, but more frequently at the Weigh-house Square, and there they exhibited in 1841. In front there was exhibited large paintings of various wild animals supposed to be shown alive inside, and a long platform, part of which was occupied by a brass band. From the street there was a staircase, by which the public were admitted to the menagerie. One of the company generally described the various exhibits, and there was often an exhibition of the training of the lions in the lions' den by the trainer. Along with the large number of vehicles, there was generally accompanying them a few smaller ones in which were exhibited freaks of nature, such as dwarfs, men without arms, who did their writing and held the pen by their toes, six-legged sheep, learned pigs, peep-shows, and other attractions at a low charge. It was a popular belief, among boys generally, that taking a cat to the menagerie for food to the lions would secure admittance to the show.

(James Leatham)

The Bonnie Lass O' Bon-Accord.

IN MEMORY OF JAMES SCOTT SKINNER

👉 "The Strathspey King", Allanvale.

144

THE WONDROUS WIZARD OF THE NORTH

A "keek" at a letter "frae Humphrey Henkeckle, egg-cadger, caickleden", concerning his trip to Glasgow. How his friend, Gibbie Goosegabble, Creel-Cooper of Gandergoozle replied, is not recorded.

Humphrey had his doubts about going to the Wizard's Magic Palace by the City Hall: "The Evil One", they a' cried oot, "Na, Na, a finer gentleman ye nivver saw; nae dealin's wi' infernal imps has he. For while his jugglin' tricks ye think ye see, performed by virtue o' his magic wand, 'tis a' dexterity and sleight o' hand; an' as yer gauin' tae stay in toon a' nicht ye'll jist step ower wi' us an' see the sicht: 'Twas altogether gorgeous, grand and new—the curtain rose, the wizard soon appeared, at sicht o' whom the audience loudly cheered, an' as he to his matchless work began, my een ne'er saw a finer lookin' man. His boxes and his vessels a' arranged, he quick as lightnin' their contents exchanged; then wi' his magic touch, as swift as thocht he wine an' water frae ae bottle brocht—poured oot dark port, licht sherry, brisk champagne, an' when at last he did the bottle drain, he broke it and brocht oot whit made me stare—behold, a snaw-white handkerchief wis there, whilk frae a lady he had lately ta'en, an' locked intae a widden boxie it's lain. He turned a lemon tae a guinea pig, made half-croons in a tumbler dance a jig, restored burnt ae-poon' notes an' ladies' sheen, and boiled doon oranges tae livin' dows. I wat it wis a curious sort o' fun, tae see him shoot a gowd watch frae a gun, syne frae a target wheep that watch awa', baith hale and soun' wi'oot a crack or flaw . . . gat up neist morn', gat a' my affairs are settled, took breakfast, gat my guid auld beast weel fettled, took tae the road, arrived a' safe at hame, bit ever since I deem I'm scarce the same, as very lately I was wont tae be; for still the wizard at his wark I see, an' spite at a' my guid freends micht say, I hae mi' doots aboot him tae this day".

(Whatever his motive, John H. Anderson left instructions in his will that a glass aperture be left in his coffin lid. His headstone is still standing in St. Nicholas' churchyard . . .)

WELLINGTON PLACE
From Union Place to South Bridge

FROM UNION PLACE to South Bridge. The south bridge is still in existence, and crosses over the Howe burn. Union Place has become Union Street, and Wellington Place has transferred its allegiance to a road joining South College and Crown Street; so now the great road south (Holburn Street) runs from Brig O'Dee to Union Street.

WESTBURN ROAD
From Hutcheon Street to Anderson Drive

NAMED AFTER the burn of the much-depleted Stocket Forest, which still flows in the open, through the remaining croft-lands of "Silverhillock". Stepping stanes, and fresh water cress, in the vicinity of the water splash, attracted bairns, who played in "Sheepies Brae". "Bonny"muir and "Hose"field, like "The Cocket Hat", were all field names, so when darkness fell, only a glimmer of candle-light could be seen in the tiny windows of Ballgreen Cottage or Raeden Farm, up its shady "Lovers' Lanie". The name of "Mastrick" Dairy Farm, likewise no longer in the country, came about when its former owner traded with merchants from the Dutch city of Maastricht.

The village of Loanhead lay on the other side of "common" pastures, that provided grazing close to the granite quarry, on the stony ridge of Rosemount. This open tract of land was referred to as "Glennie's Parks" until the eighteen-seventies, when the Civic "Faithers" created "Victoria Park".

The names of the mansions of Westburn yet remain, even though "Westburn Park" is now in public ownership, and the pavilioned country seat of "Woodhill House" has been replaced by an office block which resembles a castle keep. The house where the firm of Washington Wilson produced lantern slides for export has gone too, and what stock was left allegedly lies buried under concrete in the extended grounds of Westburn Park.

WOOLMANHILL
From Schoolhill to Steps of Gilcomston

"SEND FOR the doctor,
send for the nurse,
send for the lady
with the alligator purse."

Midwives hastened to expectant mothers from the Hospital, carrying their black bags. Sometimes their patients might be on the doorstep, for prior to extensions being carried out to Archibald Simpson's original building, there existed Garden Neuk Close. At 37 Woolmanhill, Joseph Robertson was born of humble parentage, and graduated at Marischal College at the age of sixteen in 1825. He became curator of the Historical Department in Register House, Edinburgh. On his deathbed, at the early age of 56, he declared that "I have steered my bark for a fair harbour, and found myself wrecked at the entrance". His work on archives, history, genealogy, topography and literature didn't fall on stony ground.

In olden time, so we are led to believe there were bleach fields in the vicinity, and the woolmarket lingered on till the 1850's.

Woolmanhill.　　Royal Infirmary.

"Cunninghar Hill" Hospital, called after the Broad Hill conies.

147

 Neptune Terrace.

YORK STREET

"From Wellington Street to the north side of the ship building yards"

TWO SHIPYARDS once occupied the entire length of York Street. Although Hall & Co., and Hall Russell & Co. were neighbours, and similar in name, they were independent of each other.

Handcarts trundled heavy items from the blacksmiths' shop across the cobbled street to the yards.

Some of the loons in the Boys' Brigade trundled handcarts in hard times to the Gas Works at 5 am, to obtain cinders in scoops for a few pennies. They raised money by selling kindling in cake tins for a halfpenny. Pictured with them is the Rev. Dr. Charles Cadell MacDonald, otherwise known as "C.C." David Grant, composer of "Crimond" and other psalm tunes, was a member of Fittie Kirk, 1833-1893; so St. Clements was noted for first performances.

The city dairies delivered milk down York Street, and on one occasion, Mr A. J. Fraser's horse bolted with the cart, which it left behind in the narrow space between the lifeboat sheds and the back of the houses. When caught from the oncoming waves, Mr Fraser gave the horse the necessary shock treatment by riding full tilt out to the Brig o' Don and back.

Tutesie's Mina sold sweets at a shoppie in York Street, and recalled that when business was slack, took baskets with biscuits, "fatty bannocks", and "London buns" down to the old Dee, where the "yollies" landed their catches.

York Street's pantiled houses and the fenced bleach greens at Waterside of FootDee. The arches of whole jawbones ripped from whale carcases on their way to a nearby boilyard look new; tame reminders of the stench in this district.

AT THE HEAD OF ABERD...

ABERDEEN HARBOUR

THE QUAYS

BETWEEN 1623 and 1659 were extended Eastwards towards FootDee. In 1770, the council commissioned Smeaton to construct the North Pier. Improvements including the Victoria Dock were the result of leadership from Provost, Sir Thomas Blaikie.

SHORE BRAE
From Shiprow to the Old Quayhead

AT THE foot of which was the fourteenth century quay. In the sixteenth century, the crane was used for ducking and death by drowning was carried out in a deep pool known as "The Pottie". It may be this folklore tradition that named the Shiprow lavatories, "the forty pots".

Children came to see the candlelit ships even on bitter nights, and were convinced that they saw "members of a crew of Lascars scantily clad, creeping along the decks carrying pannikins of water for an occult rite" as the candles burnt down and dropped into the murky water.

The whaleboat berth, South Market Street, where the Denburn enters the Harbour required constant dredging because of pollution. Despite the smell of wood, tar and paint, the stench was intolerable.

"The Quay-Heid", looking towards the Weigh-house, and Exchequer Row above. The Shetland boat, *St. Magnus*, is moored.

150

DOCKGATES

"THE LONDON RUN" took thirty six hours, and departed twice, weekly. Anchors lay on the ample granite quay near the steamboat berth, and boys dodged round bales of fragrant esparto grass while hotel touters in black suits and caps cooly attended to portmanteaus, carpet bags and hat boxes. Street porters assembled for work five yards away from the edge of the wharf as prescribed at Waterloo quay, beside the London boatsheds, wearing Scotch caps and harness, more familiar to travellers in France and Belguim. They took back burdens of 1½ cwt and pushed weights of five hundredweight from the quayside up to Castlegate. Polished granite, bricks, ornamental cast iron, boilers, agricultural instruments, chemicals, combs, woollens, winceys, tanned skins, carpets, candles, paper, pens, whisky, beer, brushes, rope, sails and provisions for victualling ships, a wide variety of exports for a city the size of Aberdeen in Victorian days, made this a busy port.

The French gunboat the *Cuvier* came in the 1870's for the protection of French fishermen engaged in the great summer fishing. A chorus was sung on deck at night, as with their Dutch and Highlander crews some eight-hundred herring boats put out at sundown along the harbour fairway.

On Sundays, the training ship HMS *Clyde* was open to visitors, when rows of cannon and racks of burnished cutlasses were on view. Here there were green peas, tomatoes and asparagus on board; workaday ships smelt of fish, tobacco and Scotch broth.

In autumn, a schooner known as "the aipple shippie" came into port with chippit apples from the Channel Isles; small quantities of her cargo were fished out with a rusty "dabber" and taken away in baskets, or even handkerchiefs. Sweet tasting Spanish locus beans for cattlecake were shovelled into hoisting tubs with wooden spades, and children looked for them on the quayside, where the hooves and horns of the Highland oxen, Cape and Tibet buffaloes lay in large heaps, destined to become baronial cutlery, umbrella handles, combs and pipe mouthpieces.

THE FISH TRADE

FISHMARKET PORTERS started work at 3 a.m., and the buyers were there wearing tan coloured overalls to view the fish before auctioneering started at 6 a.m. The first to buy the catch of a boat returning from her maiden voyage was presented with money to buy a new hat.

On windy days, fishmerchants' labels left on the wet fish would scatter around whilst the skippers instructed "a thin wee man called 'The Sparrow', who wore a blue raincoat polished with fishscales, to take home their fries in a yellow oilskin bag". Porters, who wore clogs, had theirs conveniently protruding from their pockets in a flat cloth with a knot in the top, as they sat alongside the lumpers at the Market cafe, eating large quantities of buttered rowies after the fish had been swiftly taken out to the fishcarts.

"The Bon-Accord" commented that in March, 1886, an odour prevailed in the old fish Market, so strong that it could restore an Egyptian mummy to consciousness".

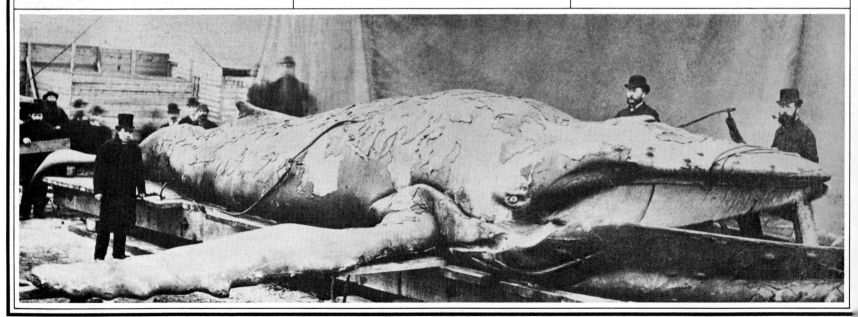

FINNAN HADDIES, FRAE ABERDEEN.

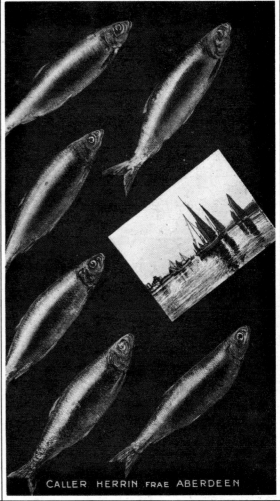

CALLER HERRIN FRAE ABERDEEN

"The Greenland Whaler's Sang"

"In eighteen hundred and twenty four, on March the eighteenth day, we lifted our sail tae the top o' the mast and to Greenland bore awa' brave boys, an' tae Greenland bore awa'."

 The hump-backed whale awaiting dissection in the vicinity of South Market Street, 1884. Folk were later invited to take tea inside the rib-cage.

"Deckies" awaiting cast-off.

Young apprentices were often told "to keep the male fish separate from the female fish", or maybe "see that the cat and the dog fish aren't fighting."

All differences were forgotten at the fish porters' picnic, when everybody was said to be "the fastest knife alive."

"The Deckies" might come from Fraserburgh, Peterhead or Aberdeen, and a ballad tells of their courage on high seas.

"Three times roun' went the gallant, gallant ship and three times roun' went she, three times roun' went the gallant, gallant ship and she sank to the bottom of the sea.

Then up spake the little cabin boy, and a fair haired laddie was he, 'I've a mither and faither in Aiberdeen Toun, and tonight they will greet for me.'

Then up spake the captain o' the gallant ship and a fine looking man wis he, 'I've a wife an' a bairnie in Fraserburgh Toun and tonight they will greet for me.'"

Horses working from dawn till dusk for their masters who established their own businesses, such as ship chandlers, foundries and fish houses, all built on land reclaimed from the estuary of the Dee.

"For men must work and women must weep though the Harbour Bar be moaning".

"Fit'll we do wi' the herring's heid? We'll mak' it into a loaf o' breid".

Pickling and speeding the smokies before firing in oak chips. All fish on the table have to be tied by the tails in pairs.

"The Killees," back of Mansefield Road.

"Flooks" to make flounders and smokies. (Smokies were made from haddocks.)

Women sang as they pickled the herring:

"Doon at the old fish yard
the lassies are working quite hard;
by the style of their hair,
and the clothes that they wear,
they're driving wee Aelikie mad.
Wee Aelikie's cursing them blind
for the work that they're leaving behind
by the style of their hair,
and the clothes that they wear
doon at the old fish yard."

The fish "Box Pool" staff.

Skinned dogfish were laid on the top of fish boxes. Three or four sold for a penny; the poor got a large turbot head free, at Aberdeen Fish Market.

Not a hair out of place?

The title of this postcard, one in a series on Aberdeen Fisherfolk, published by an Edinburgh firm, is "Morning Work in The Fish Market". However, no self-respecting lassie would care to be seen wearing a fancy scarf or a neatly pressed striped blouse while lifting fish.

155

"TORRY — OLD AND NEW"

Now . . . don't confuse Torry with Old Torry, as people born and bred in both places won't be long in telling you the difference. You may have noticed the difference in accent of Torryites and folk from "over the water". Old Torry's 3.6 acres were cleared in February 1974, leaving Abbey Road, Fisher Square built in 1870. A small rowing boat used to take folk over from Old Torry to FootDee. It was nice to see all the houses painted different colours. They looked so clean. One of the houses had a wee shop in their front room, and children on their way to the Bay of Nigg used to buy things for a picnic. By the time you reached Torry Battery you were ready for an ice-cream at the wooden hut there — then on, past the fog horn and the light house and down the hill to the other wooden shoppie. It was one continual "eat" until we reached home again".

> "Mummy, gie us a penny doon,
> here's a mannie comin' roun' —
> wi' a basket on his croon,
> selling okey pokey."

Before the diversion of the River Dee, Torry women walked to the Gallowgate with salmon nets on their shoulders. Nets were mended on deck till 2 or 3 p.m. on Saturday, and wages weren't handed over until there was satisfaction; whereupon cook shouted "money o", which meant that work was finished for the weekend, and skipper laid out the money on the table. Young members of the crew living at home were handed out sixpence spending money from their wages.

Maggie Gray sold "calderdelse" from a creel covered with a "bonnie white toolie".

The extent of Old Torry is indicated by "The Leading Lights." Ferry Road led to Petrie's Inn before the deflection of the Dee 1869-1873. Skulls were unearthed there years after the bodysnatchers fled from St. Fittick's Kirkyard.

"Awa back in the time of the widden bielers", "a man'l", "dolly tub", and basket for "huddin' the lines", in a traditional washhouse. Dry toilets were emptied by a farm hand, who obligingly left "a bag o' tatties".

James Craig baits the lines outside his home at 35 Wood Street in 1932. His yawl, 261A fished for Mackerel; *Pansy* was moored near the Leading Lights. When going to sea, he didn't get to bed if the lines were not tipped.

Many a quarrel about whose day it was on the green broke out amongst the wifies.

"My mither and your mither
were hanging oot their clothes;
my mither gave your mither
a dunt on the nose.

The old gables of the fishermen's houses faced the sea, but the windows looked onto courtyards. The wooden sleepers of "Jock Freeland's Shorie" also provided a safe haven for a crew, if vessels got caught "Going o'er The Bar" in spectacular seas.

Ships' carpenters called their houses after ports that they had visited, but babies were named after the doctor or the minister.

A FITTIE FISHERWOMAN'S SONG

"We brak nae bried o' idelty
doon-bye in Fittie Square –
A' nicht oor men toil on the sea,
an' wives maun dae their share.

Sae fan the boats come laden in,
I tak' my fish tae toon,
an' comin' back wi' empty creel
tae bait the lines sit doon.

Fa wid be a fisherman's wife
tae run wi' the scrubber an' the knife?
It's a doon-ruggin' life –
an' it's up tae the mussels i' the mornin'."

 First of three "Leading Lights"; St. Peter's church cross being the third.

SOUTH ESPLANADE WEST

From Victoria Road to Craig Place

JAMES OGILVIE'S BOATYARD was a feature of the South Bank, between Victoria Bridge, and the Wellington Chain Bridge. Mr Ogilvie lived behind the yard in "Deebank Cottage", and the fleet of "boaties" numbered some four hundred. Orders included flat bottomed boats for duck-shooting from the Duke of Hamilton.

The Ogilvies participated in the Dee sailing races, and were noted for their gallantry in saving lives.

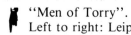

"Men of Torry".
Left to right: Leiper's Dod, Sam Gray, Cushnie and Mary's Joseph.
Kersey Cloth, "Fearnought" trousers, "cornbeef coloured" sarks, and sleeved waistcoats for "Reddin' up" were their "workin' claes". Wheelin' wool was worn next to the skin, and sou'westers of double cotton painted with three coats of linseed oil were also home made.

James Ogilvie senior and James Ogilvie junior, eel-catching on the Dee in 1890. ("They threw back the little eens".) Mr Ogilvie holds up a "ripper". It was not unusual for there to be 1 cwt. of eels lying some nine inches deep in the boat, so they wore wellington boots to avoid being bitten by sharp teeth when they "shook out the old bunch of nets which lay three feet from the surface, or emptied the traps."

SOME OLD SAYINGS about the River Dee.

"A mile o' Don's worth twa o' Dee, except for salmon, trout an' tree".

"Fit's the Dee?"
retort:
The Dee's a river . . .
if ye fa' in ye'll mak it bigger".

"I could rattle up
the rubbie dubbie Dee
to the best amangst them a'."
(an excerpt from the Drummer Maid ballad.)

Both banks at "The Foords of Dee" were worked at night and day by the fishers during the week, from February to August. When the water was low, nets could be fouled by Scots fir that had been submerged on the downward journey from Glentana to the pierhead shipyards.

Men mid-stream covered the spars with stones and gravel, crying "boat" when a catch was sighted. It was a "steady job" for pensioners "to go the nets". Needle, shuttle and twine were handed out from the bothy, and if bairns were at their granda's house when work commenced, it was difficult to escape through the door because of the nets getting repaired.

William Ewen, far right, on the foreshore outside his Girdleness Bothy, with fellow salmon fishers, 1920. The family farmed a croft at Nigg, having migrated from Montrose.
John Ewen, who wrote:
"O' weel may the boatie row
that fills a heavy creel,
an' cleads us a' frae heid tae feet,
an' buys oor pottage meal",
was a Montrose man himself, and had connections with Aberdeen.

When the River Dee was frozen in 1895, a horse and cairt were driven across the ice, without mishap.

'TWIXT DEE AN' DON

"This ae nicht, this ae nicht, the mirk an' the dawn atween, yon bairn he weers the Gordon plaid, an' his een's the eagle's een;
He sings as he gangs by the College Croon, he fustles it ower the faem, a queer auld tune til a gey auld tune, I'm thinkin' my bairn's won hame.
For it's 'Brig O' Balgownie, black's yer wa', wi' a mither's ae son an' a mare's ae foal, doon ye sall fa'."

An exerpt from "George Gordon, Lord Byron," by Marion Angus.

"Ferry me across the water,
do boatman do."
"If you've a penny in your purse then I will ferry you."

Silent braes by The Brig O' Balgownie.

TILLYDRONE ROAD

From Chanonry to Tillydrone

HEAVY HORSES hauled the pulp carts up the steep brae, past the Motte. The giant slabs prevented wheels from sinking into the mud. Aul'ton men in search of a wager came to Seton Park where horses raced.

College students played at the ancient sport of worrying the life out of the sacrists. This actually happened to one Downie, who expired after a mock trial and execution. The man's commemorative cairn originally stood

"The Wallace Tower" near the thorny knoll of Tillydrone. This dark tower originally housed a snuff shop, then a bar in The Netherkirkgate.

at Berryden, but like the adjacent Wallace Tower, both are at Tillydrone today. An inscription reads, "I cannot tell how the truth may be; I say the tale as t'was said to me." Another "claik", Peter Butter, The Aul'ton Tavern keeper, was given the treatment too, as this rhyme records:

> "They took a man, an' killed him deid,
> an' stappit him in a holie;
> Buttery Wullie, Buttery Wullie,
> Buttery Wullie Coley."

A Riddle
"Why did Tilly drone ?"
(Retort) "Because Kitty bruised her".

(Kittybrewster and Tillydrone were at one time rival rural communities.)

The Grandholm Mill Song

"Come auld and come young,
come dark and come fair
that work in 'Granum' Mill;
the denner time's roun',
and the work is pit doon —
time tae be climbing the hill.

Frae Seaton and Hayton
the lassies and lads
they Clog along back to their hames;
and sit doon for a while
then rise up wi' a smile
an' gang back to work on their frames".

*composed by Stanley Robertson,
for the photograph of
Granum Stair at lousing time.*

"Downie's slaughter" cairn.

162

Those who stayed in Tanfield, Cotton and Printfield had to cross over water on their way to work at Grandholm Mills.

The riverbank was virtually houseless, and led not to school – Bairns used to climb under the girders of Grandholm Bridge; to them, the great river valley of the Don resembled The Amazon with its rapids, waterfalls and submerged logs that looked like crocodiles floating down stream.

Pauper boys, who were employed at an early age in the Woodside Works, lived in a grim looking fortress known as "The Barracks", which was locked every night with a large key. As a child Stanley Robertson thought of them as he watched the mill workers at their daily routine from the branches of a beech tree that jutted out over the riverbank.

Only a part of the Port Elphinstone Canal survives. This ditty captures the atmosphere down on the tow path, back in those sunny, never-ending, summer days.

"Hey, haul away
we'll haul away together;
away, haul away
we'll haul away Joe."

PERSLEY DEN

Not only St. Machar himself but humble working class poets have been alone with their thoughts along this stretch of the Don between Grandholm and "The Grove".

In wartime and in peacetime, Persley Den's beechwoods and lovers' lanes vie with the Brig O' Balgownie as fondly remembered trysting places.

"I'M WINTIN' AWA BACK TAE THE AUL'TON"

"Gie me the Auld Toon,
fortune wi' his shearin' heuks
devalls at the sicht o' my goon
an' my birn o' beuks.
Gie me the Cauld Toon
wi' its noddin' neuks".

*An excerpt from "A Doric Gem",
by Dr J. M. Bulloch.*

The Aul'ton seen from The Boathoose Brae. The brewery chimney, along with a carpenter's yard made way for The Taylor Building.

THE AUL'TON MARKET STANCE

AS LONG AS a man stood with his horse for the duration of the Market day, the stance could not be claimed by the University. For many years a solitary figure defied them, but the day after he didn't turn up, trees were planted to enclose the fields.

Two ancient fairs were held here annually, as custom decreed. One, on the day before Good Friday, was a cloth market known as "The Skyre Thursday Fair"; the other being "The St. Luke's Horse Market", held in October. This was also attended by the market caravans, where a two-headed boy, a boneless man, and a fat lady took part in the entertainment. John Thom, the Town-Crier, announced the roups and the raffles.

BOATHOOSE BRAE

From Great Northern Road, over the Aberdeenshire Canal to the Aul'ton Market and College Bounds

THIS WELL WORN peat track was used as an approach from the west to old Aberdeen, by the folk from Kittybrewster Cot-toun, who helped out at the hairst when the surrounding fields yielded barley for the professors' private stills.

The Port Elphinstone flyboat berthed at The Boathouse (where the railway now runs), and on the day of The Aul'ton Market, folk made their way down to the cattle and horse fair. "Bairns off school, held the working horses' bridles for saxpence." Bargaining was slow and hard, snatches of conversation might be overheard, such as "Foo much are ye needin' fer yer horsie?" (retort), "Ah weel — gie me ten shillings". As the buyer walked away, he heard the bridle being taken off by the other "bodie", so knew that he would not have to give ten shillings for it.

CHANONRY

From the High Street, via Tullydrone Road to Don Street

THE ANCIENT LAYOUT of the Aul'ton Streets has been likened to a hangman's noose — the long High Street and a strangling circle of Don Street plus Chanonry. The symbolism doesn't stop with this disclosure, for the River Don is shaped like a shepherd's

The portrait of "The Orphan" by Sir George Reid, shows "The College Loft" where 'Varsity Folk worshipped in the days when King's College Chapel was in dis-use. The West Gallery of St. Machar's Cathedral was referred to as "The Common Laft".

crook, or more properly a Bishop's crosier. The stern words of the Church and the Law, which were ruthlessly enforced, have left in their wake a number of ghost stories. The Chanonry is still an eerie place, but at the time when the Burgh shared a policeman called "Sudden Death" with the Cot-toun of Balgownie, gas lamps were placed at considerable distances apart, and only lit during the darkest months of the year. A

Old Annie of "The Beggars' and Packmen's Free Hospice, "Redstone".

student was left reading his books by "the haunted house" that stood adjacent to old Machar churchyard, one evening at sunset, because he had agreed daringly to stay there all night. In the morning, he was found, a raving lunatic.

The Aul'ton boundary walls enclose a remote and forgotten past; and they are built of large boulders, with sloping copes. The Aul'ton was never regularly walled – Gardens terminated in earthen "head-dykes", which together formed a defensive enclosure – At the street outlets were "gates" or

"ports". The Bishop's and Chanonry Gate (otherwise known as Cluny's Gate) formerly stood in Don Street.

Country parsons lodged in the prebends' manses close to the cathedral. Some twenty of these dwellings, with their garden grounds known as "little taills", have now disappeared.

The dining room at David Mitchell's Old Maids' Hospital in The Chanonry. Spinning and knitting were considered respectable occupations for the ladies.

COLLEGE BOUNDS

From Spital to High Street

STUDENTS WEARING tattered gowns bowed their heads in learned tomes as they passed by, ignoring horse and cart alike.

From a summer house on Hermitage Hill there was a fine view of the Aul'ton, and the three powis mansions – set in their own policies – graced by mature trees.

After sunset, few folk would venture near a blocked-up gateway that still has the arms of Bishop Elphinstone set in the wall, on College

Kings College Chapel, 1883, photographed by E. Geering.

Bounds. This led to the old parish church of St. Mary of the Snows. There have been no recent internments in the small cemetery, so consequently the huge awesome figure of the great keeper of the Grave is occasionally seen. Aul'ton lads and lassies still maintain that the "Powis is haunted, I don't care what you say . . ."

The rural aspect of the place is there for residents to mind on in the names of Orchard Lane, and Orchard Walk – Beside the Firhill, near "The Thickets" stood the "Gibberie Wallie" where the gingerbread lady sold her morning bake. The Powis Burn flowed swiftly past.

The minarets of Powis, are said to have been built as a mark of respect for Lord Byron's bid to free the Greeks from oppression. Cabbies, however, pointed silver topped whips in the direction of the ironwork, decorated with a crescent moon motif, and told tourists that Turks still lived there. To the bairns it was simply "many towered Camelot".

The Hermitage, which stood on a sand hill, was removed for its gravel deposits in 1926.

Bairns clambered along the high dykes or called to each other at either end of "Powis' Whispering Wall".

The starved corpse of Earl Leslie, dressed in "hermit's claes", was found here, according

Powis Gates. ("Many towered Camelot".)

to David Grant's "Ballad Romance of Olden Times."

(This saddening tale, points out Stanley Robertson, has a better known precedent in the original version of "Lord Gregory", otherwise known as "Annie O' Lochiryan".)

Both lordlings die of remorse, but the prophetic moral of the ballad comes from Mary Hay's father, who said that if his daughter, "The Flower of The Don", became Earl Leslie's common-law wife, it would mean "the winnin' an' the brakin' o' her hert".

Powis Lodge minaret.
The Laird was an admirer of the Byron cult.

The Hermitage of Powis; a once familiar landmark of the Aul'ton.
From this vantage point, the early vistas were delineated by engravers, prior to the invention of photography.

The Hermit of Powis lived in his cell,
And shunned the converse of man;
His food was the coarsest, his drink was the brook
That near to the Hermitage ran.

He mumbled his prayers, and counted his beads,
And scourged his flesh wi' twine,
In the hope to atone for the sins of the soul,
By the body's dool and pine.

He prayed, and starved, and scourged himself,
Till his lean frame leaner grew;
But at last the curtain dropped on the scene,
And then the truth we knew.

*An excerpt from "The Hermit of Powis",
by David Grant, 1862.*

The Snowkirk (St. Mary of the Snows) was dismantled in 1640, "to repair decayed chamber windows and construct college yard dykes". The University further ruled that the beadle of St Machar's cathedral was not to open the ground until £8 for the privilege of interment was paid into the King's College coffers.

The Birdies by the Gibberie Wallie "jist ran back a bittie" when old Bawbie Courage fed them on "foostie breid and stale parley cakes."

King's College Library's ceiling is shaped like a galleon. This was just as strange a land to the layman as "Treasure Island".

DON STREET
From St. Machar Drive to the Old City Boundary

THE OLD BEDE HOUSE (1676) is still considered fine and warm because it has thick walls. Just inside the door, is the blocked-up underground passage to St. Machar's Cathedral, which could still be walked through within living memory. A story is told of how the beadle used to buy the minister's booze, at the grocer's shop by the Townhouse, and smuggle "a carry out" into St. Machar's, where the two of them would have a good dram. Evidence of this was found in the old passageway, which was nearly blocked with them throwing empty bottles down it.

Buchan carters halted at the Black Nook alehouse by the Salmon fishers cottages to find out who was receiving "salmon money" from the charities, or maybe marvel at how much money was in the Bridge Fund.

Although there certainly are a good number of poems and tales of bewitchment associated with Richard the Mason's "Brig" — "By the Brig O' Balgownie I'll meet ye — bonnie Scots lassie o' mine" – this was a trysting place for lovers, and the walk in the shady lane is still there waiting.

Grant's Place (1732), at 80 High Street, used to have a clutter of coal sheds on one side of it; and on the site of the MacRobert Memorial was a cabinet-maker's workshop. He was perhaps the only witness when the River Don changed its course.

The Bede House. Until 1786, the Bedesmen lived at Bishop Gavin Dunbar's Hospital, which stood adjacent to St. Machar' Cathedral.

HIGH STREET
From College Bounds to St. Machar Drive

CABBIE GRAY, at his stance outside the Town House, "wore a black velvet jacket and shepherd tartan trousers." He, and the shop keepers who stood at their doors when business matters didn't press, watched the brewery horses setting off to Balmoral on a two-day journey, laden with beer barrels for Queen Victoria's household.

Before the coopers went to work in the morning, they met in St. Machar's Bar for their breakfast of small beer. When the brewery closed, they sadly looked at the engraved lettering in the mirror that still confidently advertised an establishment that was larger in area than the original college itself. The sound of their hammers and those of the granite workers in the nearby yards often reverberated against the freestone walls of Kings. Causewayers paved the Aul'ton Wynds, and were seen coming back to check their work on the Sabbath. Danger lurked in the closes such as Mackenzie Place and Thom's Court, when bairns played there, because heavy carts trundled past on their way to Donside Paper Mills, laden with pulp.

Women came round the doors selling "caller dulse", and fish from their creels, but there was bargaining going on in the shops as well, and when a thrifty farmer's wife came in from Buchan to her favourite drapers to buy maybe a shawl to keep out the wind, on being told that it would cost twenty shillings she would make to leave, indignantly remarking, "twenty shillings man, ye're surely nae at yersel' – Na, na, we winna deal the day if that's your price." "Come awa" was the retort – "Ye're nae gaun' awa' that wye, look at the quality of the colours – at a pound its cheap; as ye're nae everybody, I'll mak' it eighteen shillings to you".

"Na, na, the quality and the colour's right eneuch, it's the price that's wrang, but as I

High Street looking towards the Town House. Two courts on the right led through to Dunbar Street. One contained the Free Kirk manse and the Soup Kitchen, the other was Greenlaw Court. When the soup kitchen was emptied, squatters moved in, and at first wouldn't vacate because the college officials who had plans to restore the building. The only answer was to demolish the building around them. Work was indeed started, and they had to flee for their lives.

The world of the academics was considered to be a backwater. The tone was set by Bishop Elphinstone, "who had improved the singing in the quire of St. Machar's Cathedral," and had given much thought to the fittings, ornaments and ceremonial at King's College Chapel. His memorial, which now stands in full view of passers-by, was submerged in the Grand Canal at Venice before it could safely be transported to Aberdeen in peacetime.

"The Ivy Tower", somewhat overshadowed by Old King's Library, and the brewery on the other side of Regent Walk.

hinna time to look aboot, an' as I get a' my things here, I'll gie saxteen shillings, that's mair than I can weel afford" – "Weel I wid be delighted to gie ye it at that price if I could, but at eighteen shillings ye're getting a great bargain, so I'll better jist roll it up to you" – "Na, na – nae ae penny mair will ye get fae me – tak' it or want it."

The salesman, knowing that the value of an article is just what it will bring, escorts her back from the door, and tells her not to tell anybody the price she paid for it; her bargain is thus concluded.

Dealing men were often needing an extra item as their "luckpenny" if "siller" was handed over the counter.

REGENT WALK
From Dunbar Street to Aul'ton Links

THIS, CONFIDENTLY states the Post Office Aberdeen Street Directory, appears to be the case. A cassied stretch of the road, which originally cut through to High Street past the Manse on one side, and the brewery on the other, still exists. This is due to the Aul'ton folk rising up against the College (as they had done on the occasion of the ruination of the Snowkirk) and telling them not to close it to traffic; so an archway, built in 1912, still gives pedestrian access to Regent Walk.

SCHOOL ROAD
From the Knackers Yard beside the Links to the Town House, old Aberdeen

THE SHOOTING RANGE was near the salmon fishers' bothy on the Links, and flooding occurred in winter – whereupon, Aul'ton lads and lassies skated round the hillocks and islands.

Sometimes, they would help to herd the cows up the road, and on one occasion a beastie got stuck by a downpipe behind the townhouse, in a narrow alley called "The Needle-ee" – six pushed one end, and six the other – with eventual success. The fire

Isie Stewart was the best "wheeper o' bottoms", in School Road Schools.

engine, which was kept in the ground floor of the townhouse, stood in readiness. At the time this happened, carts had to come up School Road, round the townhouse to get to the Chanonry, because the cottages at "The Needle-ee" stood in their path. Now St. Machar drive has, like a camel, found its way through "The Needle-ee", past "snowball's hoosie", now more properly renamed "Cluny's Port".

(Just prior to this photograph, of what now is St. Machar Drive, being taken, a neighbour had rushed across to the garden wringing her hands and somewhat distraught: "Could she jist pit up maybe twa duddies tae dry? It's nae my day on the green".)

SPITAL
From King's Crescent to College Bounds

AT THE "Froghall Plotties" coal "cairters" bred canaries in "pidgeon lofts" – ramshackle sheds held together by corrugated iron, and tin advertisements.

By the light of a hurricane lamp in this alternative university, Aberdeen terriers with grey hair on their backs were boot-polished for prospective customers.

Tea planters and shipmasters made St. Peter's cemetery (built over the site of the Spital hospice and chapel), an impressive place where stone angels stand sentinel.

THE PUB CRAWL

by W. J. Buchan

There's plenty pubs in Aberdeen
Frae Torry ower t' Mastrick
And I have been in maist o' them
My stomach's something gastric.

"The White Cockade" – nae lemonade
And "Gleggie's" famous "Cellar"
To "The Grampian Bar" – and that's nae
    far,
I've drank wi' mony a feller.

"The Waterloo" – were I've been fu'
The "Neptune" doon in Fittie
And "Simon's Bar" whar mony a tar
Goes lookin' for a bittie.

The "Empire", "Club" and "Bon-Accord"
And of course – "The Tartan Divie"
For mony a rare nicht I've spent there
Along wi' Snuffy Ivy.

There's "Paterson's" – "The Waverley"
Aye – even in the "Tiv"
Wi' half a dollar in my pooch
An' dressed up like a spiv!

A nip an' a pint in "The Union Bar"
An export in "The Lorne"
A strong ale in the good old "Crit"
Forget about the morn!

I've struggled in "The Hop Inn"
Survived in "The Royal Oak"
That's a helluva place tae ha'e a glaiss
It's nae for gentle folk!

I've dragged my feet up Union Street
and nipped in tae "The Grill"
a glaiss o' rum an' a packet o' crisps
Oh I like t' ha'e my fill!

"The Star and Garter's" just roon by
"The Palace Bar" as weel
I've stood there aye till closin' time
And staggered oot fair feel!

"The Frigate" for a pint o' stout
"The Henhouse" for a laugh
"The Wallace" for a game o' darts
An' a pint o' half an' half!

"The Coach and Horses" – Friday nicht
Or upstairs in "The Swan"
I like a bit o' sing-song
Tae wash doon my Black an' Tan!

There's "Allan's Bar" in George Street
Sit doon tae pie and peas
"The Balaclava's" my next stop
I'm nearly on my knees!

Then "Winter's Bar" – "The Northern"
And ower tae "The Crag"
'Twas there I nearly foonered
As I shoved awa' a bag!

But onward to the "Butcher's Arms"
There's nothing like a crawl
For booze is jist the very thing
T' keep awa' the cauld!

"The Stag's Head" roon in Hutcheon Street
Last stop afore the club
I've nae much cash – I'll ha'e a slash
A handy thing – a pub!

Well here I am hame again
Now whar the hell's my Key?
The wife – she's waitin' wi' the boot
Tae hear my latest lee!

Wi' the thockt o' a' this wallop an' wine
I'm feelin' kind o' merry
So I'll awa – but mind at nine,
I'll see you in "The Hairy"

"Sawdust" Calder, supplier of sawdust
to bars and butchers. He was also
referred to as "The fiddler frae The
Forest o' Birse", where he stayed in his
youth. During his years in Aberdeen, he
was better kent as "a puir aul' cratur".

AND NOW . . . A FEW BARS

GEORGE BERNARD SHAW referred to Aberdeen and her bars in his play "Candida". Even Shakespeare, who is said to have visited the city in October 1601 with his fellow actors "was minded 'on" by the name of a now defunct bar in Marischal Street. Robert Burns' local was the New Inn adjacent to the Old Tolbooth.

Lord Byron (some say that his early years in the city make a boring read), was drawing upon childhood observations of his "ain fowk", (whose love of poetry, a quick word and a pithy repartee is still undisputed), when he wrote ". . . and so our life exhales – a little breath-love-wine-ambition-fame-fighting-devotion-dust, perhaps a name." Some of the fondly remembered names of the lost legion of bars echo his belligerent sentiments: "The Hairy Bar" (East North Street), "The Artillery Arms" (Queen Street), and the "St. George" (Schoolhill).

Saturday night was a peace-offering time, when a man might buy his wife a new overall, as well as taking home fish-roes, chips and a halfpenny poke of peas. Children waited hopefully by the door of "The Royal Oak" to be taken late night shopping in nearby Castlegate. The light of carbide lamps, the patter of marketeers and impromptu concerts were just as exciting as an occasional fight, when women would object to a "bobby" interfering, and tell him "to leave that wee mannie alone, you great oatmeal monument".

Oblivious to these "carry ons", old men peacefully smoked their clay "dodies", and chewed black "bogie roll". Young men who leaned nonchalantly against the mahogany counter saw more than they would admit reflected in the engraved mirror, that confidently advertised a long defunct brewery.

Hefty men were on the "cairties", rolling barrels onto the straw-filled sacks, and loading them into cellars with stout ropes. Their drink was bottled Bass, and some drank the dregs as a laxative. Others preferred a "black draught" drunk on the spot at the chemist's. Apprentice barmen wore aprons originally made from white flour-bags that were boiled up to remove the ink stains. They were smoothed out by "combing the fringe", but when they were "time-served" could afford the wing collars and bow ties.

At the Pilot's Inn, Foot Dee, Jinsie Smith let early morning customers take their breakfast drink at 6 am. As she knew them by their tread, she would only get up from her bed if a stranger came in. The sound of clattering feed bags woke up late risers who lived by "The Bridge of Dee Bar", whilst the milkman took his 10.30 tipple of rum and cream. (You had to put the milk in first then add the rum, otherwise it would curdle.)

Pitch pine, which was used to fit out the workmen's bars, could be seen emerging from ships' holds at the harbour.

Fish market workers found it a thirsty job piling up tons of dried and cured fish, and quenched their thirst accordingly; however, "The Brethern fishermen" were practically

"Well of Spa" Bar, at the corner of Spa Street. This popular meeting place was a landmark in Gilcomston. The Denburn used to flow past this front door, under nearby "Collie's Brig".

teetotal, but felt "a heap the better for a glass o' rum as a bolster for gan' o'er 'the Bar', and it also benefitted bodily ailments such as a cough or back trouble more if they seldom let it within their lips". If asked to have anything then it was, "Weel . . . I'm T.T. in a kind o' wye; nae bigotted ye ken; I never took ony pledge. A man's aye best that can templar himsel'. Aye, I'll drink a health, no' that I care a brisk pint for't. Nae thanks, I never tak' water; that's what the lions and tigers drink." As a half a gill of 33 overproof that could peel the back off a granite monument vanishes, the only indication of what has happened being a silent tear stealing down a weather-beaten cheek.

Donside carriers who took a drink at the top of long George Street needed "a wet when it was dry, and were dry when it was wet". Whisky at "Split the Win'" was washed down with spring water.

"Sawdust Calder" belonged to Birse; and in his homeland of the Dee, was recognised as a talented fiddle player. The sawdust he delivered to butchers' shops and bars soaked up the blood. It has been said that the "East Neuk Worthies" resembled members of the tarot pack (and that included Calder, who sadly ended his days "a puir aul' cratur").

When country folk departed from a friendly pub in Commerce Street, the landlord was sure to say "Peep, peeps – see youse in Brechin".

When moletrappers went out for the evening, they "dressed swank". Their hand-stitched moleskin trousers were made from skins that had been stretched on wooden pegs, and rubbed in salt. Travelling men sold horses' hides to the knackeries, where skins were soaked in brine, then salted and dried in steaming heaps. It was not unusual for a skin to be taken forty miles by handcart; the man between the shafts (his wife and bairns keeping the skin company in the cart).

"Crown & Anchor" Bar, Regent Quay.

177

Sandy is a sailor lad
bides in Ferryhill
Gets his pay
and he buys half a gill –
come a ring come a King
come a tarrybag,
come a ring come a King
come a tae.

"Johnnie, he's raise,
and he's pushed the door open,
crying 'cursed be this tavern
that ere let me in – and cursed
be the whisky that mak's me sae thirsty.
Fareweel tae ye whisky,
for I'm awa hame'."

*An excerpt from the ballad
"Johnnie My Man".*

"We'll hae a blaw o' the leaf, an' tae
hell wi' the bairns."

Label from "Long Bar", Castlegate.

"Mither MacDonald's" Bar, East
North Street.
"The guid statute of the Toun decreed
that it sall nae be lesum tae ony
hostilar, tavernar or vintner of wine or
ale tae sell or vint ony wine, ale or
beer aifter ten hoors at nicht, at whilk
hoor nichtlie the college bell within the
Burghe sall ring."

Devahna Brewery staff and cooper,
1898.
It was said that the coopers were,
"Mighty bare armed men who with
their heavy hammers, oak staves and
metal bands made and repaired casks.
Work might proceed with greater spirit
when the heat of the sun produced a
few good drams from the wet wood."

THE INVERSNECKY PHOTOGRAPHER
from the Singing of Harry Gordon

I used to be the barber for the toon an'
    roon aboot,
Till a bargain sale o' safety razors knocked
    my business oot,
But I had messed sae mony people's faces
    up, ye see,
That I thocht I'd be successful if I tried
    photography.

Chorus:
Moisten the lips wi' the pointie o' the
    tongue,
Dinna look as if ye were expectin' tae be
    hung,
Try and wear a pleasant smile if that be in
    your power,
And watch for the birdie an' the hale thing's
    ower.

Examples o' my talent in my window are
    displayed,
I've got the local belle wi' a' her dentures on
    parade,
I've got Hillie's man wi' an expression like a
    scone,
A bride wi' plenty muslin an' a bairn wi'
    naething on.

THE YULE EVE SANG

    "Rise up guid wife an' be nae sweir
    tae deal wi yer breid as lang's yer here;
    the time's ill come fan ye'll be deid,
    an' want naither meal nor breid."

Harry Gordon — "The Prime Minister
of Mirth" — in his cornie shoppie
sketch.
His character songs were "as popular
as gramophone records", and the
Inversnecky series included the Doctor,
the Bellman, the Bill Poster, the
Fireman, the Lamplighter, the Smith,
the Barber and the Beadle.

"Weel, weel aul' Aiberdeen,
A something there's aboot ye
That grips wir hert an' weets wir een.
We couldna dae withoot ye:

Some folk they say ye're unco ticht
An' keep yer siller oot o' sicht;
But, Lord be here,
They're far fae richt,
They simply canna ken ye."

Patsy Gallagher had a news stand, and
wrote his own headlines. He wouldn't
"swick onybody, and naebody wid
swick him". The bill boards on one
occasion read "Winston Churchill in
Dundee, Patsy Gallagher in
Aberdeen". He also sent telegrams to
the Queen. Replies concerning the state
of her health were pinned up for the
information of his regular customers.

An' when he came tae Aiberdeen
The English Fleet it wis lyin' ready
Tae carry him doon tae Edinboro' toun
Tae catch the lad in his tartan plaide.
King fareweel, hame fareweel,
A' tae bid oor King fareweel.

An excerpt from the Jacobite Ballad,
"King Farewell"

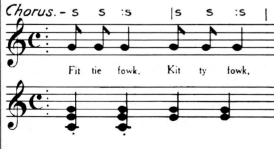

Chorus.- s s :s |s s :s |

Fit tie fowk.   Kit ty fowk,

m .f :s .m |r .d :d

coun try fowk, and ci ty fowk,

181

STREET NAME INDEX

Italics denote photograph of subject

West North Street meets Queen Street. ☞

Family businesses had their warehouses in the vicinity of The Green. Falconer's covered waggon is about to hit "the cairters' trail oot o' Toun".

Customers' shoes were uplifted by this vehicle; one of a fleet of delivery vans, that serviced departments in the Co-op Arcade, Loch Street.